So Late into
the Night

Elinor Nauen

Rain Mountain Press
New York City
- 2011 -

$15

ISBN: 0-9802211-4-5

The cover image is *Untitled (Nocturne)* by Will Yackulic. Used with the artist's permission. From the collection of the author.

Author photo by Jadina Lilien.

Library of Congress Cataloging-in-Publication Data

Nauen, Elinor.
  So late into the night / by Elinor Nauen.
    p. cm.
  Poems.
  ISBN 0-9802211-4-5 (pbk.)
  I. Title.
  PS3564.A8736S6 2011
  811'.54—dc22
                         2010054101

Designed by David G. Barnett/Fat Cat Graphic Design
www.fatcatgraphicdesign.com

Rain Mountain Press
68 East Third Street, Suite 16
New York, NY 10003
www.rainmountainpress.com
info@rainmountainpress.com

FOREWORD

For many years, my husband and I have spent our summers sitting in parks, reading long poems aloud. Taking turns, stanza by stanza, we've made our way through *Paradise Lost, The Prelude, Omeros, Paterson,* Thomas McGrath's *Letter to an Imaginary Friend,* among quite a few others. The one long poem that wouldn't let go of me, or that I couldn't let go of—even after we'd read it aloud, and I'd read it to myself, and reread it—was Byron's *Don Juan.*

I remembered that mad John Clare believed he was Byron and had written *Don Juan, A Poem,* so I dug that out. It's not very good, lacking the fun, wit and humanity of Byron's poem.

But it gave me the idea to try my own response to *Don Juan.* So I wrote a stanza of ottava rima, the 8-line stanza that makes up *Don Juan,* as well as Byron's earlier, shorter (and delightful) *Beppo.*

Boom! One stanza was all it took. Love at first sight. I instantly knew that ottava rima was what I was going to do from now on. From the first stanza I wrote, I could see that those eight lines, with their a-b-a-b-a-b-c-c rhymes, was infinitely flexible and could contain, shape and propel everything I could possibly want to say—narration, social commentary, description—in a persona I could both reinvent and stay true to. I knew I would discover more and more ways to live inside this form.

And so it proved. I kept going (and going and going). Every morning for a year, I got up and wrote a stanza in my notebook. For a long time, that's all I did. I wrote about whatever caught my interest that day, without a plan. I fooled around with meter and topic. I walked around in a fog of rhymes. Someone would say an unusual word and I would automatically try to rhyme it.

Eventually, when I started typing up the stanzas, I noticed that I was writing about the same things I always write about—baseball, road trips, living in New York, being from South Dakota, my husband. And gradually, over several years, the poem took its present shape.

I also read up on both ottava rima—which was used variously and successfully by Auden, Yeats, Kenneth Koch and Pushkin, among others—and the long poem. Which I didn't even know I was writing, because I had in my head Philip Whalen's remark that the way to write a long poem is to go to the same bar at the same time every day. (Which I am surely misquoting or misattributing.) Writing a long poem is different in many ways from writing a short lyric. The length itself is an element of the poem, exactly as it is in very short poems. There's the fact of living with one work for years. There's the extras you develop to keep yourself interested: I had a great time stuffing the poem with acrostics, footnotes, haikus, a poem in Middle English, the rules to an elaborate card game my sister Varda and I invented, and a few other tricks.

And then one day, *So Late into the Night* was finished. I reluctantly and happily leave it alone from here on in, as soon as I have expressed some thank yous.

Acknowlegements

Parts of this work have appeared in very different form in the following publications: *Booglit, Court Green, The Corpse, Hanging Loose, RealPoetik* and *Skidrow Penthouse*, and at the 36th International Congress on Medieval Studies, Kalamazoo, Michigan. I am grateful to the editors.

Thanks go to Blue Mountain Center and many people connected to BMC, for the gifts of time and attention: Ben Strader, Harriet Barlow, Sheila Kinney, Chris Marzec, Helen "Sis" Eldridge, Diane McCane, interns and fellow residents; my family, including cousins and courtesy cousins; Jack Collom, Maggie Dubris, Marion Farrier, Bonnie Goldman, Dr. Joan Haahr, Kathleen Hamilton, Marlene Hennessey, the late Jimmy "Beau" Kousar, Maria Mancini, Albie Mitchell, Tim Morris, Murat Nemet-Nejat, Alexandra Neil, the late Roberta Oliver, Maureen Owen, Danny Peary, Bob Rosenthal, Douglas "O'Malley" Rothschild, Abby Sosland, Rebecca, Emma and Jake Stowe, David Trinidad, Tim Wiles and Mark Zussman. Eileen Myles contributed encouragement, careful reading and a lifetime of friendship. Even more and evermore, Johnny Stanton, who I can't believe I could love more than I do, but I do, every day; and who tolerates what I say about him.

TABLE OF CONTENTS

DEDICATION

"Writers don't give prescriptions — they give headaches!"
Wrote Chinua Achebe. Well, I'm giving
Myself one. Is life nothing but earthquakes
Blue roiling the placid, unforgiving
Shallows? Will I never get some death breaks?
I always choose the highway of living
But it feels like the road is neatly greased
Into the dominion of the deceased.

And so to dead friends and loved ones I hurl
All the life I can stuff into this poem. Beau,
Doug, Elspeth, Uncle Clifford, Uncle Earl,
Auntie May, Danny — and that's a salvo
From just a couple of years. This sad girl
Hates to lengthen the roll by listing row
After row from the Rolodex of the Dead.
I'm happier when there's joy to be spread.

PRELUDE

Deciding "no" is more evolved than "yes,"
Says William James, as it takes a greater
Element of inner labor. With less
Work one goes along, rather than take a
Stand. How to tap our deep resources? Eff-
Ort, ideas and excitement make us
Come alive. Despair lames most people though
A shipwreck can form a surprise hero.

An unpredictable future — I'm so
Taken with that phrase. Bearable present
And unpredictable future, the goal
Of my attempt to appraise incessant-
Ly my life: motives, crimes, lapses, sorrow.
Is it a bearable, if hesitant
Past I hope for? I'd like it to recede,
Filed like tax returns, no audit; no weed

Poking through the smooth, cultivated lawn
I have endlessly tried to embellish
With pleasantries. Where is the past? Long gone.
It *is* the tax man. It's the mole relish-
Ing the holes only seen in the blunt dawn
When I rise. My life's not so much hellish
As heckish. Is it less deleterious
When I'm being flip or when I'm serious?

Electricity — now, there's a subject,
Like it or not. Me, I don't like it much.
I confess I feel nervous and object,
Not to talking about it, but to such
Other acts as plugging in imperfect,
Rubbishy appliances. I'm touchy:
Nasty, devious electricity!
Author of shocks and much duplicity!

Unlike electricity, I like fish.
(Even though my sign is Aquarius;
Note: its symbol is electric waves.) Wish
We had vegetarians quite that serious,
Rejecting swimming creatures as a dish
Or guarding their rights. Eating fish rarely is
Thought of that way. (Only cows are deemed cute.)
Eventually, fish-lovers will be less mute;

They'll make the casual dining world see
Harming fish equals anti-animal rights.
I would like to quote Lord Byron here. He
Said, "No angler can be a good man." He bites
Perhaps more than he can defend? Surely
Others concur and have reached the same heights.
Enough! It's time for us to sally forth
Making tracks for the fun we'll have henceforth.

I. PO' WORLD

"O Ocean, Ocean — salty, cool and green!"
And why not grab a line from Kenneth Koch?
He who in *Ko* served up so many scenes
Of baseball, cars and kiddies drinking coke,
And though these are subjects on which I'm keen,
My characters don't drink but snort the coke,
My baseball's more full of butts than his and
My cars don't drive on boats but only land.

Although Byron's my model more than Koch
I honor Kenneth and his fine rima,
His daintiness with color and a joke,
His ability to go to Lima
In the middle of a poem on a cloak
Of folly that is in fact a schema
Of sensibility and sense un-sour.
O Kenneth! O Koch! Yon poetic power!

If only I could learn to fling a rhyme
To the educated cognoscentis
In the formula of Stephen Sondheim
Or the half-forgotten Ogden Nash. He's
The master of slipping extra words into four/four time
And pulling off silly insoucientis
That well illuminate modern mores
In sophisticated, pointed, esprit de corps ways.

I throw down my patience in exhaustion
At most verse. "Of all the ineffable
Centaurs that were ever begotten
By Self-Love upon a Nightmare" — laughable
Byron's thought (and capitalization)
Maybe, but who wouldn't give half a Wool
Carpet to Proceed on Lines that will hold
A Reader up more than the blank, un-bold

Creatures that skulk throughout much of today's
Poetry — skimble-skamble who no doubt
Have always hung round what can be a maze
Of peculiar puzzles, ones that a lout
Can be as enclosed by as one who pays
Benevolent notice. Being devout,
Alas, is no guarantee of talent,
Insight, success or enlightenment.

Perhaps you'd like to hear more of Byron —
My master, my love, my poet, my guy —
And the traits that draw me to him: iron-
Y, for one, as modern as any high-
Tech gadget, and as assured. The siren
Allure of sympathy, thrills and sex. Why
He's not everyone's fave poet I don't
Get. He isn't for anyone who won't

Admit humor and human narrative
To the pantheon of poetic purpose.
Outraged by amoral imperative,
Some spurn his work, as though to disturb us
With the life is to taint the heritage
Of the writing. "The life's wrong, a circus
Of immorality, therefore the po-
Etry's bad." Scratch *that* as fatuoso.

A birthday stanza: me and Byron, pair
Of Aquarians, although he was doubtless
Less stuck up about it. I'm Februar-
Y 18th — today, as I write, though less
Sure it'll be when you read this unless par-
Allel rivers rush you into the dress
Of celebration. It's your birthday too?
Call me at 555-6142!

To sit at a French bistro in Soho
Drinking good hot chocolate, reading baseball
News (at last!), gazing as fat, fluffy snow
Lofts past the window, wearing my new shawl —
Could any birthday have a better mo-

Ment? Not mine. Bob Rosenthal told me all
Aquarians love their birthdays. That plus
Love — ah. It was a great day — lots of fuss

From lots of friends, but always the right sort.
Everyone knows their own parameters
(She says ungrammatically) — I court
Then freeze off attention. A meal, glitter
Gifts, a cake (but no singing waiters!). Your
Perfect day is perhaps more amateur:
You may lie low, want only your best friends
To know and no one else. Aquarians tend

To have hundreds, so we don't throw parties
Unless we have lofts and can entertain
Everyone. To triage does not please;
To leave out any pal makes us complain.
But *now* I am sitting in a skeezy
Waiting room, the doctor hours late, in pain,
Made worse by the annoyance and the puff
Apologies I'll receive soon enough,

And tres sad: Everyone in the world will
Have a birthday before I do. Shall I
Name names of birthday overlookers? Spill
The beans on my shit list? They don't know my
Birthday is my occupation? Jill,
Bill and Harry, fuck you six ways to Fri-
Day. It's easy, pal: There's Opening Day,
Valentine's Day and — not least! — my birthday.

A birthday is the coolest date in town.
So democratic — you can't be so poor
You pawn it, nor so rich as to nail down
An extra. It's one to a customer!
An anniversary is differently wound —
It takes two. Or so I thought, though rumor
Has it my mom lately celebrated
Her fiftieth with my dad long since "late."

Dream Haiku: T.S. Eliot
at a colony
snooty, wouldn't read with me,
no apology

And now I get to write my "have arrived"
Postcard from Blue Mountain Center. Hurray!
I'm here! For a month! All that time to dive
Into books, my poems and (in my own way —
Gingerly) nature. Adirondacks, five
Hours from home. A month off work! Plenty play.
Even though I expect to be hard-nosed
About this poem, none of that is imposed.

What I'm doing here: Blue is what is called
An artist colony, where writers et
Al — painters, musicians — spend a month walled
Off from the world, allowed to concentrate
Exclusively on their art. We're fed, mauled
With solicitude, waited on, cosseted.
Meanwhile, back home, spouses and loved ones
Are saving up resentments and shotguns.

You can eat well here at Blue from sunrise
Till the loons come home: eggs, sausage, bacon,
Oatmeal. That's just breakfast. Let me apprise
You of the cookies, fresh daily, achin'
To be crammed into your belly. Some guys
Have gained as much as thirty pounds — makin'
Food their main work. Sis (the cook) is no doubt
Happy. If you don't eat, she says, "Get out!"

Today I took a short hike (.1 mile)
Through the Cathedral Pines, past Racquette Lake
And majestic pines that had somehow, while
Woods were being clear-cut, missed being taken
Down. A brass plaque to World War II flier
Malcolm Blue rested on a stump "as straight-
Grained as he." Flowers, flags. What would it be
Like to back a war with the whole country?

16

Didn't see a bear out by the dumpster
(From an Old English word denoting "judge").
No, wait, that's not dumpster, I meant dempster,
Which back then was dispensed with a cudgel.
Dempster is married name of a friendster
From high school. How did I manage to budge
So far from the bear of Blue Mountain Lake?
I saw a bolt of sun, mist in its wake.

One warm night here in the Adirondacks,
A woman swam far out into the lake.
Then lonesome Mormon melodies cracked
Through the fog in high tremolo, slake-
Ing such sorrow as comes from the long smacks
Of ancient joys. A fair woman naked
In unseen water, wreathèd sounds wrapping
Pines, loons and me in weary calm, capping

A night of wine, hilarity, earnest
Film discussion, frivolous inquiry
Into politics, state-of-the-world mess.
I have been around too long to worry
About grand themes, to blaze in the furnace
Of burning issues. Or is the jury
Still out: Can we ever dig up something
New or is echo always on the wing?

My interests don't fling too wide. Luckily,
Cars and baseball fill multiple stanzas.
As you will shortly find out, they must be
Two of the richest fields east of Kansas.
The poets could go on about these sultry
Things alone and there'd still be bonanzas
Of metaphor and meaning for the next.
Cars and baseball are big as death and sex.

Dream Haiku: Philip Whalen
"I dreamed about you last night."
"People often do—
I must be an archetype"

17

Let's try again. Who else might I scribble
A line to? I do like the notion
Of saying "Dear Blank" in this poem, Sybil-
Like attention in every direction.
Portmanteau poem that holds every quibble
And arrow of insight and promotion.
I need a shot of you, Lord Byron, here
To flutter round and draw honey from... dear.

But it's not that simple. What do I call
You? If I bring you forward to my time,
It's George, I suppose, or Byron. My gall-
Ing informality'd be wiped out, I'm
Sure, two hundred years ago. Okay, doll,
Clearly I need a pet name or I'm stym-
Ied before I begin to write. How did
Auden address you? He probably slid

Over that and now I can't find his book,
Which is likely at my office. Just as
Likely, when I'm there I'll forget to look
For it. Okay, anyway, hi. Lust has
Its imperative and I want to fuck
You. Wait, I mean, I simply want justice
Here: Why'd we have to be born two centuries
Apart? Would I've had a shot? Censor me

In this but desire comes hard on the heel
Of admiration. What's a poem for but
Sex? The pure poets of America squeal
Or I do, out to have a good time, cut
Some games and fun into the deck, then deal
Out a hand of Crazy 8s to the sluts
And poets. Slip-slide along, take a good rest
Or swim, leave your heart untorn in your breast.

Speaking of Wystan, did he use a rhyming
Dictionary? I wonder if I can steal
A couple of his end-rhymes. His timing
Is pretty darn good too. His thoughts more real
And lofty than mine, his poetry chiming

With medieval artists, while I reel
In butts and baseball. Hang on to your beer,
Ladies, I'm gonna hafta get smart here.

Recent enthusiasms: medieval
Poetry, old sports cars and Derek Jeter
(Who gets his own section). An upheaval
Would be to examine him and deter-
Mine what brainy background might bedevil
His fine backside. His brains may well teeter
But Jeter's athleticism is smart. He
Can't explicate music; he's not arty.

Saw exhibit of photos by Eugene
Atget. (Couldn't use his name as end-rhyme —
I'm not sure how to pronounce it. I mean,
French is so darn tricky.) I liked best (I'm
Predictable) his industrial scenes
And cities. For trees I'd give not a dime.
Photography is not my favorite art —
Without words, no medium truly has heart.

Know that Thurber story about a guy
Who stepped out of character just one time?
Made a woman go crazy with his lie.
Everyone believed *him*. It's not a crime
To change! I only now see how unli-
Kely it is for anyone to divine
Why people are or do what they are or do.
Was that ungrammatical or just stu-

Pid? By and large I take pleasure in where
The rhymes propel me but they can be abrupt,
Encouraging quick conclusions that snare
Truisms and/or silliness that corrupt
The plump, stately, grandiloquent air
A long poem must display to erupt
Into epic status. Yes, Kenneth? Right,
Byron? You agree majesty makes might?

Actually, they are the last two (I'm third)
Who think that. More accurate mottoes for my
Poetry daddy-o's might be: Gloom's a turd;
May as well glorify as mortify;
Or: solemnity is for the birds.
Their poetry can be one big Versailles
Full of panoramic clouds, daffodils,
Mirrors, cornets, dishabille and dactyls.

Dream Haiku: Professional
Ed Sanders asked me
to edit his latest work:
$100

One thing about being in your for-
Ties is you give up presenting an es-
Capee face (unless it's your true one). For-
Tunately, you quit caring that you as-
Pire only to know the new cars and score
Of yesterday's game. Your inner boy as-
Cends, your inner snob dwindles. What was it
That Marx said about capitalism? It

Will soon wither away? Similarly,
My pretensions have been reduced, and I
Admit "all she cares about is the Yankees,"
As a John Ford Noonan one-act that I
Saw had it. The main character barely
Could go out. She stayed in her house to cry
For the Yankees. I like to get paid, for
Everything except poetry. Stay poor

And know it's pure. "If no one is buying
The bread you bake, you can make it as salty
As you want," said Nemet-Nejat, tying
His Turkish philosophy in with Walt
Whitman's embracing, unfettered flying.
Why be poor, when it is such an assault
On dignity and health? That is, without
Money. Poor is different. *That's* about

Access. Access to jobs, to folks with cash.
Wealth means one can afford indignation.
John Steinbeck said that you can dress in trash
Only if you're rich and on vacation,
Or too poor for it to matter. Your pas-
Sion has to be tempered by your station.
That is, having something to lose marks
You as an impure follower of Marx.

Product placement! I said to Dan Mullen.
I'll put you in my poem – your daughter Eve
Also! — for some ready cash (a million?).
Dan mulled it over then stood up to leave.
He didn't cough up so I got sullen.
Yer outta here, pal —

It's also tough to stick to poetry
If you're getting plenty money and praise
In other ways. For me, it's not solely
The perks of journalism, though the ways
It buoys one are many, from a low glee
In being nosy to evoking days
And friends of one's youth, plus hilarity,
Conversations and even clarity.

That's valid and will be absorbing not
Just today but ongoingly. Why is
That not a word? Ditto "Lierati,"
A Scrabble adaptation I'm a whiz
At (since I co-invented it). You've got
To fabricate plausible words, then mis-
Appropriate meaning. The words have to
Be real English. No stringing the X, Q

Or Z. It's not Polish scrabble! I re-
Call boytoy and weefy. Luckily, Dot
Documented the Lierati we
Played. On request, I will dig out that shot
From the piles of photos and junk that de-
Spoil my office. Lierati is not
For the competitive but ideal for
Those who like the words better than the score.

Years ago, my sister Varda and I
Invented The Great Game of Bingelbumpf *,
Which is played with two decks of cards, sly
Maneuvers and e'er-shifting rules. Harrumph:
Another million-dollar scheme unlike-
Ly to net me a penny. The triumph
In Bingelbumpf is getting over —
Sister beating Sister. We're in clover!

Don't you wonder how you'd do on *Jeopardy*:
Get flustered or answer as well as you
Do at home? I notice that hardy
Players, like athletes, ignore a miscue.
Jeopardy is an old people's party —
The ads are for cholesterol meds, flu
Shots and the like. Oddly, many ads don't
Name the problem they solve. Do they not want

---

* Bingelbumpf is a game for two players, using two decks of cards, ideally with identical backs (two blue decks or two red). The object is to be the first person to get rid of all your cards, which gives you a letter toward spelling the word B-I-N-G-E-L-B-U-M-P-F. Whoever first spells out Bingelbumpf then gets a "big B" toward spelling out another meta-Bingelbumpf. Ad infinitum.
    Deal seven cards to each player. Turn up one card to start the discard deck.
    The nondealer goes first. She can choose to follow suit or match by number (jack on jack, 6 on 6). If unable to play a card, she draws up to three cards then passes. You are not required to play a card, as long as you draw three.

Special rules:
    If Player A puts down the 2 of hearts or the 2 of spades, Player B draws a card either from A's hand or from the deck (the choice is A's). If B draws the queen of spades, A gets a letter toward BINGELBUMPF. This rule has no name.
    The 3 of diamonds is a *rimmerman* (technically, a *marvin rimmerman*). This is a wild card rule. You may, for example, require the other player to instantly switch hands with you. Any rimmerman must be invoked *before* picking up your cards. Another rimmerman (this doesn't require a card, actually) would be to require both players to talk in funny accents for the duration of the hand. No more than one rimmerman every dozen or so hands.
    All 7s are *speedbumpfs*. If Player A puts down a 7, Player B has to pick up two cards, unless B also has a 7, which cancels A's. But A can re-cancel, and so on. The last 7 is the operative speedbumpf. After picking up the two cards, if the player cannot put down a card to keep game in play, she must then draw up to 3 more cards before playing or passing.
    An 8 changes the discard deck to the suit of the 8. Note: You cannot play the 8 of the current suit; for example, if spades is being played, you cannot play the spades 8.
    James bond: If A plays a card and B has the identical card (suit *and* #; for example, the 4 of clubs and the 4 of clubs), B plays her matching 4, saying *james* and may play another card (as long as it's allowed, a club, say or a 4) saying *bond*. If you have the matching card but not a legal followup card, you say *clouseau*. Note: Use a very fakey English accent for these terms.
    Uno: You have to say uno when you have one card in your hand. You have to say it *the very instant* it is true or suffer dirty looks and rude personal remarks.
    Doppelgänger: If A goes out and B has the identical card (cf. james bond), she lays it down, announces doppelgänger and A has to pick up three cards – the game is *not* over. Ha!
    Forgotten rules: *fujitsu, fujitsu; menage a troy-troy-troy.*
    The names of all rules must be announced when invoked.
    If you get to the end of the deck without a winner, shuffle the discard deck and begin again. Return the queen(s) of spades to the deck. If the queen(s) of spades is(are) the only card(s) in your hand, you have to draw three more. You cannot go out on a 2 of hearts, 2 of spades, any 7 or any 8. You *can* go out on the queen of spades.
    Note: Bingelbumpf is a constantly evolving game. Do not assume that these rules are fixed. Suggestions for improvements are welcome.
    Note: Swearing is allowed.

People to know what's being sold? That's fine
Except how do you know if you need them?
How can you ask your doctor for "Lermine"
Or "Pirivent" with no clue to the fem-
Inine or allergic need they're to line
Up against? Into the promotional tem-
Ple of medicine we sidle on faith,
Bolstered against appearing like a wraith

Or turned into one. To a peddler, change
Is improvement. Even if happy, you
Should be someone different. The real danger
Is settling. There's a pill for that too.
As they say, life is the problem. The strange-
Ness and disarray need to be regu-
Lated. It's a funny thing about pills.
I'll pop 'em for pleasure but not for ills.

T— talked about pills like oenophiles go
On about wine. He'd discuss provenance
And the most subtle effects: the ammo
Attack of this, the gradual ensconce-
Ment of that. Some people I know would stow
Away every pill from Providence,
Where they all seemed to come from. You mean guys
Will give me drugs because of my big ... eyes?

         《《—》》

Hard by are a dozen books, all of which
I'm reading this minute, though some have lain
Unopened long enough that they are itch-
Ing to move to "forsaken," not the bane
Of a book's self-love but where it can bitch
Undisturbed by flighty readers who feign
Interest. One-night stands, as it were. Heed
Joyce, who said it should take as long to read

His works as it did him to compose them.
A book can be read in just a few hours,
But to write? It must take longer to em-
Broider even the most plain. I devour

The fruit of planning, planting, pruning; gem
Of mining, milling, machinery. Ours
Is a life made in every way so easy,
It's hard to see what pains are made to please.

Today is the birthday of Lord Byron
(Sam Cooke as well, another of my guys).
I'll write why I find him so inspirin'
(Two Aquarians, heavens!). To versify:
The siren of wildness, the environ-
Ment of frolic and wit (Cooke's throaty sighs,
Shivering runs), the plain-enough diction,
Smart allusions and dead-on depiction

In his characters and types. What seems mod-
Ern is his worldliness, though he's often
Mawkish, without falling into slipshod
Gush. It may be that's what I can't soften
Toward, since I get patriotism and god
Aplenty from earnestoes quaffin'
Deep drafts o' death while they sneer at success
And the American style of excess.

Just spent an hour reading Byron's letters —
With pleasure, but also some despair
That he'll always be among my betters,
The coolest kid who deigns to share the air,
Slugger who slights Punch-and-Judy hitters,
Superstar disdaining peons who stare
As he motors past in his creamy Jag.
Byron disregards from a dreamy crag.

If this were February, it'd be
March by now. Nice to be born in that short
Month. Name origin? I'm blank. I can re-
Call the others (not May) but am thwarted
Of recall to sidle over and de-
Liver Feb's past. As kids we were exhorted
To "look it up!" every time we asked
A definition or fact. Hence, my fast

Progress toward the household dictionary
(Or encyclopedia, depending),
Where I discover that February,
In ancient Rome known for representing
Purification, in ordinary
Times had twenty-nine days but surrendered
One to August. In her low-cut bodice,
Maia was Rome's fertility goddess.

"And what is so rare as a day in June"
Was memorized by my brother at eight.
You might say, "What is so weird as a tune
In May?" "Then, if ever," J.R. Lowell states,
"Come perfect days." Our milkman in Sioux
Falls was named Jim Lowell; his greatest trait
Was that he'd give kids rides in his milk truck.
So I was not the least bit thunderstruck

That my grammar school was named after him —
James Russell Lowell School. Standing in his
Truck for a grand ride to the corner, Jim
Lowell was my idol. Surely a ride is
More fame-worthy than turning out a slim
Volume of verse, I believed, cheesehead whiz
That I was at the time. Now, of course, I gloat
That I went to a school named for a poet.

For someone who loves to study and learn,
Who was very successful in high school —
For me to so quickly, as I did, turn
Against formal education and rule
Against college may seem strange. I can churn
Out reasons: on my own at last, pure fool-
Ishness, lazy hippie and who knows, Jack,
All these could be true. An autodidact

Overcomes a lack of formal training.
You know, I did graduate from high school
And credit my teachers for me gaining

Whatever I do have of grammar rules[*]
And similar solid stuff. A waning
Number of smart dames who jump in the pool
Of teaching rather than law or medicine
Makes it doubtful that my schools — Edison,

Lowell and Washington High — are as cap-
Able now. When I lived on Flying Moose
Mountain in Maine, it was a mile walk up
To my tres rustic cabin. No lamp juice.
No water. I read Chaucer and Bishop
To my cats. When it got dark in my hoose-
Gow, I cried. I expected this would make me
A saint. But I did read lots of Shakespeare.

"Someplace in my life between 10 and 14"
Is a line I just found in Eileen Myles'
Cool for You. She slithers out of routine
And back facilely, in a book whose wiles
Are both tricky and transparent. I've seen
Her do it a thousand times, but her style's
Still mysterious and profound and mannered.
Are these the attributes she'd like bannered?

> Dream Haiku: Paul Newman
> plump & bald, he leaned
> behind Ed Friedman at the
> Poetry Project

When I first showed up at the Poetry
Project, everything was wide open. It
Wasn't Establishment but a furiously
Working school. Our entire social life fit
In its one room and spillover bars, re-
Volving among the Ukrainian, Orchid-
Ia and Grassroots. We all knew which tavern
Was in. They switched like a lighthouse lantern.

[*] What's new in the world of the subjunctive?
"Changes in grammar tend toward glacial,"
Said Jane. You thought the subject defunct? If
She's editing textbooks, I guess she shall
Set you straight. She proclaims that the junk is
Tedious, waves it away with a facial
Expression of ennui. Grammar is for
All, but talking about it is a bore.

Parties were a step up from bars in cer-
Tain ways, though you could leave with someone from
The bar more than split together from your
Apartment. More discreetly, that is. Some
Collaboration'd always be occur-
Ring at a party. Typewriters would hum
Along with Motown. Dance — write a line — dance —
Write a line. Each endeavor would enhance

The other. When the record went off,
Someone'd read the group poem. It was al-
Ways bad. The host would keep it and rip off
The one or two good lines. Then we would all
Crack up, then more music and it was off
Again with another partnered poem. Al-
Though nothing publishable may have come
From doing them, the words! the words! did hum.

     Dream Haiku: John Ashbery
     I *was* listening.
     I didn't turn to prattle
     but to scratch my back

The first time I was ever at the Church,
Which became my alma mater and home,
Was a Frank O'Hara tribute. I searched
Nervously for Second Avenue, know-
Ing the East Village was dangerous, a virt-
Ual jungle. While I'd used my thumb to roam
Thousands of miles, cities appeared absurd-
Ly forbidding. But I found St. Mark's, heard

Ginsberg. Allen Ginsberg! A famous poet!
Another person who read was a guy
Who looked like Bozo the Clown, in green coat,
Plaid trousers and fluffy reddish hair. I
Moved to the nabe soon after to go it
In verse, enrolled in a workshop taught by
Bozo, that is, Jim Brodey, who said once,
"I haven't seen any of you for months

At readings. If you want to be a mod-
Ern poet, you have to know what your peers
Are up to." That made sense, and it was an odd
Monday or Wednesday night for many years
When I wasn't at the Church. A large bod-
Y of work got written there. You had cheers
And challenge from your friends to spur you, plus
Readings you'd want new work for. Entre nous,

The main guys for me are poets: They could *talk*.
They saw in me what I wanted to top
The list: the work. Perhaps the most evoc-
Ative picture from those days would be stop-
Ping at the Church for yet another rauc-
Ous collating party. Everyone'd drop
Whatever else we weren't doing to cruise
Around a big table, assembling news

We knew for sure would stay news, in the form
Of mimeo mags. Some folks were a whiz
With stencils (fixing typos caused enorm-
Ous splotches if you weren't slow and undis-
Tracted). The paper was rough, sturdy, warm
Off the press. We were hot with drink, work, siz-
Zling anticipation: Maybe you could
Go home with the author! Not that you would

Necessarily but desire under-
Lay poetry, as it always has. Once I
Hooked up with Johnny Stanton, I wondered
Why I should write, since it wasn't to try
To seduce guys anymore. All younger
Poets have to make that shift, put lust aside
And write toward something else — like parodies
Or sports or even the damn verities.

It wasn't all rosy exaltation —
Plenty of whining and feuding as well.
Some people felt dissed if their insatia-
Ble desire for fame was thwarted or fell
Short. Some people took a vacation
From their marriage, didn't bother to tell

Their spouse that they weren't coming home. Events
Of casual sex with lasting consequence.

One time, Johnny Stanton and I went to
A reading. I looked around and announced
That I had knocked boots with six poets who
Were there. Johnny quickly confirmed my counts
By naming all six of 'em. How'd you do
That? "Easy," said Johnny smugly. "I bounced
My eye around the place, knowing you'd fall
For the best writers in the Parish Hall."

  Drinking Song

  Beetle-browed browbeater
  Undoes & undone
  The stout ale smoothes
  Under & undone

We had cheap apartments and no money
And worked as little as we could, enough
To pay the rent, buy cans of beer, many
Of which were drunk as we wrote, argued, puffed
Pot and cigarettes. We all spent minu-
Sculy on clothes. However, we looked buff
Because we were excited all the time.
Every night was a reading or some kind

Of poetry event, usually centered
At the Church. Brodey ran readings at Zu,
And we *KOFF* girls (the magazine's center-
Fold of nude male poets our claim to fame) drew
Some to our places for readings. Gender
Issues were for real, but we didn't use
That word — we just made fun of guys. My
Crummy jobs were messenger and truck dri-

Ver for a lesbian magazine-deliv-
Ery service. Not lesbian magazines —
Owned by and employing women. One viv-
Id memory is of talking my ven-
Al way out of a parking ticket by sniv-

Eling, "I got my period, you've seen
How that goes, your honor." Judge was embarr-
Assed and he shooed me right on out of there.

Paul Violi, handsome, dark and skittish,
Headed the Project. Everyone was young.
Ron Padgett, Eileen Myles, Ted and Alice,
Steve Carey and the Twelfth Street boys, all gung-
Ho about poetry. Interest diminished
For some as it got harder to stay strung
Out; not unlike a drug, poetry requires
Stamina and optimism. The lyres

Get unstrung as adult life overpowers
Unrealized ambitions. Or adult death,
Often drug-related, sad to say. Ours
Was a chemical world, poetry like meth
Or pot as altering to one's powers
And attentions as a drug. Every breath
Went straight to and from poetry. Ted would say
For a poet it's twenty-four hours a day;

All that you do is a poet doing it
And everything is necessary. Now —
Ah, skip the present for the moment. It
Is full of poetry now too, no doubt.
I mean, I'm elated by the young poets
And by a lot of those who've been around
Forever. No matter where it comes from,
Poetry's a big party. All are welcome!

After learning to write poems, a young poet
Has two other duties: to organize
A series of readings and to put out
A literary mag. You anthologize
Yourself along with a writer of note.
People come to hear Ms. Big lionized
And semi-incidentally you too.
This also applies to the mag you do.

Maggie, Rachel and I edited *KOFF*,
The main publication of the Consump-

Tive Poets League, first po-mag where men doffed
Their clothing — they were nude from chest to rump.
Some learned from Michael Lally so they fluffed,
That is, were semi-hard. Those who didn't pump
Looked, thanks to our brilliant photography,
Like eggs on a plate. Holman and Lally,

Warsh, Simon Pettet, Tom Carey, Violi,
Rosenthal, Godfrey and Simon Schuchat,
Joel Oppenheimer, Bill Kushner, Kim Chi
Ha, Bill Berkson. That all of 'em? Fuck it.
We got so sick of nude men after we
Did a calendar with twelve, we chucked it,
Though we did publish one last *KOFF* proto-
Type on t-shirts with our manifesto.*

O young poets of 1978!
Our poetry trembled with sincerity
And with smart ass-ity. We emulated
Frank O'Hara with too much verity
To the biography. We adulated
Berrigan with doubtful wit. Charity
Suggests I name no names. Lord Byron in
"Scotch Reviewers" sure did but my run-in

With friends and "English bards" seems too risky.
I can't battle pals or big guys either.
Besides, as you know by now, I've been frisky
With too many of 'em, they're bequeathers
Of many good lines, nights and tough whiskey.
I'd rather praise than scathe, take a breather
From rivalry and wallow in beauty.
Arguing isn't *always* my duty.

---

* **The *KOFF* Manifesto**
Because I am an artist, things affect me deeply & I am constantly depressed. Because an artist must be totally
honest, I can say without a trace of self-consciousness that my inability to deal with the world proves
definitively my superiority to most of the human race, yourself included. It is impossible for you to understand
even grossly the nature of my pain. In your dull way, you can only admire my suffering, as you might admire
a computer or a large, shiny car; I suffer for all of you. As you go daily to your draining and repetitive jobs, I
feel the futility of your lives. I understand without having to experience. I am the antennae of the race, & for
that reason much more fragile than those of you who make up the thick and ugly body.
—Maggie Dubris & Elinor Nauen, from *KOFF 4*

II. DEREK AND THE BOYS

Enough of the downtown scene. My apartment
Is really tiny, so let's grab a break.
We'll leave not just the nabe but Manhattan
And go to the Bronx. Yankee Stadium! Take
The 4 to 161. The first great moment:
When the train rises from the ground. The fake
Roman Coliseum startlingly looms —
White, columned, huge, imperious — a tomb

For the futile hopes of all other teams
Who for a century have suffered harsh blows
From the booming bats of the Bombers, and reams
Of great pitchers. Mantle, Ruth, DiMaggio,
Lou Gehrig, Jackson, Whitey Ford. They've creamed
Teams in two dozen World Series, whipped foes
Who have had a few good men of their own.
The '99 team was great — Williams, Cone,

And my fave, Derek Jeter, the shortstop,
Who not only hits to the awesome max
But has a grin sweet as a lollipop.
All the girls yearn for Derek, he's not lax.
But it's also true that he doesn't drop
Balls, he makes every play with grace, he acts
Swell to fans, calls the manager *Mister*
Torre, not Joe. But his big plus? His keister.

Of course, Jeter's more than just a cute ass.
For years he has been one of the premier
Players, improving all the time. A mass
Of stats proves this — good arm, hitting a "mere"
.349, flashy fielding, speed. Doodads
Like these do nicely ornament his rear.
Oh, there I go again about Butt-Man.
No, really, I'm a truly serious fan.

Women love a man who can bunt. New sea-
Son — new hits, new runs, new errors. That bat
Could be put to better use. As you see,
Baseball's full of adages and advice that
Can help a person organize and se-
Lect all aspects of life. That's why I've gat-
Thered these valuable lines from a lifetime
Of musing on the national pastime.

Bought the first daffodils of spring today.
Not from the greenmarket, so they're hothouse,
I guess; the market is strict on what ways
Goods can be included: no flowers doused
With dye, no butter from commercial dai-
Ries cut to look Amish (scandal that aroused
The scene a few years back). These daffodils,
Like baseball, bring heart to a quick standstill.

Listened to the first game of spring training.
Yanks lost but who cares? Getting that rhythm.
Sterling and Kay announcing, maintaining
The thread. Spring training for fans too, sit 'em
Down to relearn the pace of games, feigning
The knack until we get re-accustomed.
The players are poised and light on their feet,
We fans beery, unfocused but replete.

Even this early in the new season
It is satisfying to have baseball.
Hey! *Especially* this early! Knees 'n'
Arms 'n' lungs need the balmy air to loll
In, stretch in, wake up muscles. The reason
To go down South now, of course, is for tall
Sun, grass thick as snow and the reminder
And idea that life soon will be kinder.

Baseball's all about seeing. It's robust
When you catch subtleties, like spring out West —
Undramatic, you let your eyes adjust
Till you can *see* what's there. Or, I guess,
Like reading Chaucer: Once you're in focus

It's abruptly clear, after which the rest
Really is English. Likewise when you see
Jeter crouch an inch, you know he forsees

The incoming pitch and where the hitter
Is likely to punch it. I recall Lou
Piniella deemed the best slow outfielder
In baseball 'cause he knew so well where to
Position himself. As a spectator,
Once you understand that each action you
See represents a mass of strategy,
You are catching the sport's complexity.

It's like appreciating sex, which is
Like digging jazz — at first cacophony,
Indistinct sensations and sounds that fizz
At and around you. Any poverty
Of attention means that they swirl and whiz
Past unorganized. A monotony
Of information when unsorted — fun,
But not as good as when you know a ton.

Summer eve, the colors a simple scheme:
Green and blue. The stretch of grass like spring hay,
The blue of uniforms and the sky gleam-
Ing over our head. The smell's not quite prai-
Rie, but country enough to make it seem
Relaxed and with all the time in the day.
The teams get set by playing easy catch.
I draw a scorecard and prepare to watch.

Playing is a different story. Our team —
The Dead Dogs — was truly the most ragtag
Gang that you can imagine. Our Supreme
Ineptnesses gladly, gracelessly dragged
Ourselves in many merry fashions. Beam-
Ing kids pitched in as pinch runners for lag-
Gard smokers, and a dog was our most game
Outfielder. But what we had was a name.

And that's what mattered. Our priorities
Obviously weren't skill or focus, as
We played but one game a year. Sotheby's
Will never auction off *our* razzmatazz.
We held banquets too, and need more o' these.
But I suspect that's it, that we are has-
Beens as athletes and I will likely not
Become the next Yankees third base hotshot.

But in a real way, the Dead Dogs were sports
At its core. That is to say: banquets. More
People ate than had played. We gave awards:
The Oil Can Boyd Mysterious Illness for
Refusing to be alone on base. What sorts
Of further trophies? A bounty! Some poor
Schnook took home the Lenny Dykstra Slick Lips
Statuette, and there was the Chet Lemon Hips —

Okay, so it was really for his butt
(There's lots of good ones). Isiah Thomas Grin,
Lou Piniella Manager and Big Gut
(Ha ha: Neck). Eddie was ghost runner in
Quite a few cases, which meant that he cut
Out of the batter's box for you. (He didn't
Serve as pinch runner.) I remember our
Bon mots better than our baseball power.

Whatever way I go to games does please.
Solo or with a gang, good seats or so high
That squinting shows little more than a frieze
Of players in place. The times I'm by my-
Self I sometimes count every pitch — I seize
A rare chance to be compulsive. I'm pli-
Ant in a group. In manifold fashion
Can one give in to a baseball passion.

I always keep score. It's automatic.
I draw a scorecard while I'm in the throng
Rattling uptown on the train, emphatic
To see the game this way, a snapshot long-
Er lasting than an actual static

Photo. Have my own system, get stuff wrong
Lots, so wait for official decision
To mark hits and errors with precision.

I'm not bothered that I'm not all that good
At scoring, nor do I mind when I miss
Something. It's not archival. I once would
Toss my scorecards as I left the park, dis-
Regarding a perspective that could
Be personal, i.e. for my own his-
Tory in baseball. I still feel the same —
I'm in the moment at the park, not aimed

At immortality. So my scorecard
Is my memory, not the game's sculpture.
It's all right not to be guilt-tripped or jarred
Into liability, voluptu-
Ously revel without burdens or hard
Choices. I know what I know and endure
Not knowing more than that. It all makes sense
When told strategy but I don't get tense

Trying to keep track on my own. Despite
All the years of watching, I don't know much.
I remember a few facts — hits and right-
Handed pitchers, an odd catcher and such
Other random trivia as Whitey
Ford's win total, McCarver's BA, Dutch
Leonard's — uh, name. I am not precocious
(Often a synonym for atrocious).

Here's another reason that I like go-
Ing to baseball games: It's one of the few
Times when I am in a crowd that I don't
Feel alienated, awkward or su-
Perior. I want to sit in my row
Like everyone else and enjoy the view
In an unpretentious (not unintell-
Igent) way. Jump up, keep score, boo and yell.

I once inveigled Maggie on a jaunt
Up to Yankee Stadium. It was Watch Day,
Bleacher seats a buck-fifty and we want-
Ed those timepieces. In fact we were way
So poor that a free watch was worth the saunt-
Er north. I knew nothing. To my dismay,
I never had boyfriends who liked the sport —
A requirement that would, you'd think, abort

Any budding romance, but here I am,
Some twenty years together with a man
With whom I've gone to exactly one game,
On our first-ever date. I was a fan
And he knew this. Sweet and thoughtful, right? Damn!
Why did I often read his gestures jan-
Gled? So I felt set up instead of pleased.
Johnny has tricked me, I thought rudely, he's

Not here for the love of the game, and John
Before him wasn't, nor Maggie my best friend.
I asked a pal if love could come with none
Of the baseball signs. Sure, it's not the end,
He said. "Look at my wife — she took it on."
I wish Johnny and I shared this. Could he bend
Or could I move to his basketball? Go
Be a wife dutiful and yielding? No.

I'm a one-sport fan, although I'm starting
To like ice hockey. But those guys fly past
Too fast to really see how they're parting
The ice. I learned more by watching, aghast
(A little), my godson Wyatt darting
Around with the little squirts. Though they're fast
As otters, I can keep tabs on the puck
And get a sense of the whole muckety-muck.

Okay, so we've cruised on up to the park,
We've bought our tickets (your usual seat?
The seller asked) and strolled to where the arc
Of blue sky and insanely green field meet,
Scimitared by the curving of the dark-

White, roofless Yankee arches. Summer heat
Flutters as we climb up to our children-
Of-paradise seats in this great cauldron.

Note that while incorporating the -eet
Rhymes (above), I refrained from using one
That would seem obvious, that is: Derek Jet-
Er. What is a jeter? One who jetes? Done
How, and why, do you suppose? With the feet?
Does it mean something in Romanian?
It would be too cheap a shot to put here
One more aside re Derek's divine rear.

    Jeter

    Derek Derek
    Ass homeric

Is it possible that I never rhymed
Jeter with peter? My love for him's pure —
What need of innuendo when sublime
Grace informs his every move. The sewer
Is not where my thoughts follow him, not slime
But flowing grass, sun and leather the lure.
My handsome hero is Derek Jeter
I wouldn't mind a shot at his peter.

Another thing about Derek Jeter
Is his extremely excellent posture.
A back that's straight and upright. *Back*, reader,
Not bat, though his bat is on the roster
Of interesting things about this neater-
Than-neat ballplayer. I want to foster
Admiration for the fine — *very* fine —
Points of his appearance in the Bronx shrine.

When Derek once wouldn't dance at a club
With Mariah Carey, his old girlfriend,
His name became a verb: to jeter, bub,
Is to dis someone, blow them off, to end
Things coldly. This begs the question, the nub

Of which being: What did his name portend
Before he was bigger than it? To unmask
The answer, I went to Europe to ask.

Jeter's name is everywhere in France.
No, I am not seeing things! It's on show
All over: "Merci de ne rien jeter dans
Les W.C.," which means "Please don't throw
Rubbish into the toilet." What's the chance
That his name would denote "throw"? I forgo
Ze droll French way of leaving off ze last
Letter; as dumb American, I'm typecast.

How could I have forgotten it was Der-
Ek's birthday?! A Cancer. I doubt that we'd
Have much in common unless he was bare
In which case I would admire his steed
And dream of a ride. I'm supposed to care
That I have a husband, although to feed
A fantasy requires no mundane cook.
I can love Johnny and still cop a look!

Do you want to hear of the baseball strike?
Will the players and owners be able
To concur pre-deadline? I don't much like
The chances. I'm wretched. On the table:
Revenue sharing, salary cap, hike
In fees and distribution of cable
TV movies. Business. I'm cranky
'Cuz all I want is to watch the Yankees.

If I say I'm watching the seventh game
Of the World Series, you might know the year.
2001: first year in ten it came
Down to seven. It's hard to watch. I fear
For the Yankee regime, that they'll be tamed
By the Diamondbacks. Clemens is near
Trouble, two on, one out. I can't watch it.
Eek. I'm quaking with nerves that they'll botch it.

Okay, so I am suffering a bit.
I'm a Yankees fan all the way. If my
Team wins, it's groovy. But they didn't hit
A lick, field or pitch. So I'm not miffed by
The Yankees losing Game Seven. It
Has been terrific baseball. Why sniff? Why
Should I expect a victory every game
More than death, taxes and husbandly blame?

«—»

I once saw John Olerud hit a triple,
A big slow guy lumbering toward third base
But seeming not as fast as a cripple.
He'd hit double, homer, single; his race
Was to fill out the cycle. A ripple
Went through Shea when they realized. His face
Belongs on Mount Rushmore, with its flat planes
As American as are the Great Plains.

"Cuba is known for music, tobacco,
Sugarcane and baseball — four essential
Elements," said Gilberto Dihigo,
Son of Hall of Fame's Martin, quintessential-
Ly versatile, lone Cuban enshrined, no,
Tony Perez now and eventual-
Ly Omar Linares and who knows who
Else once we can go back and forth to Cu-

Ba more than can be done now on impulse
Or even by design. They have those old
Autos that make my American pulse
Beat wildly. They have shabby streets and gold
Sunsets and winter baseball to convulse
Me with delight. Cuba is a stronghold
Of imagination and desire for
Northerners gazing at that postponed shore.

Yankee centerfielder Bernie Williams
In attempting to lure Juan Gonzalez
To the Bronx spoke not of the millions

Of dollars he'd make, but of the solace
In "going medieval" — showing billions
His bat's punishing power. Causing volleys
In me would be him quoting Ethelred.
That would be the ultimate godhead.

Ran into Marlene the Medievalist
On the train, she'd been to Kalamazoo
For their convention. Do they go ballist-
Ic — or is it catapultistic? You
Make archaic jokes and dance, herbalist
And witch, student and professor too.
Our T-shirt plan: a blunderbuss tooting
At a dictionary, captioned: "Skeat Shooting."

She prefers the Middle Ages to the more
Trendy Renaissance 'cause there's less glitter.
People's lives seemed more like ours, with the poor
More solidly present in the liter-
Ature, the way the Jewish Bible (or
"Old Testament") has warts and all — bitter
Feuds, failures, falseness. In the New Testament
An idealized portrait is what's present.

What's missing in medieval lit is play,
I suppose because, as Hobbes said, their lives
Were "nasty, brutish and short" (what I say
About my husband's unpleasant ex-wives).
They need baseball! It's just that auto-da-fé,
Sadly, was the entertainment that thrived.
You can't change the past retroactively
Unless you can close your eyes effectively:

In a somer seson, • when soft was the sonne
The coche, gedraeg and heretoga • to the gamen-felde of
     baseball gonne
A hauene of habite • halewed by swete hey,
A meine riche in the reame ... • pytchers rowting reke their
     swevene.
I was were forwandred • and went me to reste
And sit by the midward-felde-gome • thrid aestandan side

42

I seigh a licht pytcher on a heigh-place • throwing ymaked
    palesye
To a betræpper there-inne • alrebest in bataile.
A faire felde ful of folke • fonde I there bytwene

Of alle maner of cnyssan-men, • the mighty and the
    mayme
Brucaning and cocking battes • as the coche asketh.
Some putten them neh the pytcher • for a claene anlepe
    pleyde.
In squatting and in swinging • swonken ther thikke alblast
    ful harde
Bifore a dampned noumpere • who deman to domesdaeg:
Hnitan aerest! Hnitan tueyne! • Hnitan alast! And oute!
Neist cnyssan-man hitte harde • to luft-felde: Home irun!

Among the watchers, • the wawe like a wal walters.
They standen and sitten • like a strand.
Neist a cnyssan-man of more conynge • clyppes to the
    comyns.
He bihotes to brothely • by-taht for the gedræg.
But the pytcher biloukes • the bryche segge in a bire,
With a fairehead of a falling sloder • fast to the egge of the
    plat.
A maistri withoutdyn mene • in midouernon,
Bitwix cleo-partie • with no hopand of speding.

      «« — »»

Which distractions are a part of the game
And which not? Cellphones and the stock market
Should be stowed away posthaste. Since you came
Here to leave daily life behind, park it
Back at the office. Watch the game. No blame
In riding off on memory train, target-
Ing an opposing player for invective
Or in putting past games in perspective.

Who's that guy pitching today for Boston?
Knuckleballer Tim Wakefield. Hilarious
To watch those balls jiggle toward home, lost in
Space like puppies in a pond. Precarious

43

In an unpredictable wind, tossed in
Most gently. Batters find them nefarious,
Curse as they swing and miss, or else they top
The balls meaninglessly to the shortstop.

Yanks finished June with first losing record
In four years. It's been horrid. No pitching.
Ledee traded to Indians — a heckler's
Dream to get Justice, *my* sort of bitching:
Admiring his looks! Have yet to check'er
Out for **ass**ets. I'm merely fidgeting,
When what you want is the panorama
Of baseball, in all its glorious drama.

The big picture is made up of the small —
Each inning, each pitch, each readjustment.
At the plate, the winning run walked in ball
By ball. It's like a DNA judgment
Done in the laboratory, crawl by crawl,
Till at the end the man's proved innocent.
Baseball's only tedious to watch before
You know what you are looking at or for.

Baseball is made up of two elements:
Short, sharp, snapshot moments — e.g., a catch
Griffey Senior elevated and bent
Back over the leftfield wall to snatch,
1985 — and their complement:
Undifferentiated time in batches,
An alt-universe where life rolls along
With simple, non-personal rights and wrongs.

Yanks beat the Sox big last night — I'm afraid
I'm going to be providing a running
Commentary this season. Don't upbraid
Me, please. I'll try to work in Jim Bunning
And his politics for distraction, grade
The science writing in the *Times*: cunning
And compelling. Bunning: conservative.
There. Let's go back to Jeter's curvative.

Derek Jeter's not the original
ButtMan, by the way — Willie Randolph has
Filled in nicely for years. A pigeon'll
Appeal with the plumpness of its breast, as
A man with fullness behind, digital
Manipulation perhaps not as daz-
Zling as the usual computer picture.
"What was the ecstasy, what the stricture?"

Tomorrow (Tuesday) I will meet Derek
For real. (Thank you, Danny!) What will I wear?
I would be less nervous to meet Bill Veeck
Or Curt Flood — more excited too, I swear.
I hope I don't giggle — I'll be a wreck
If I embarrass myself. I couldn't bear
To have to tell my friends. Plan a remark,
El, that's it; no "uh ... uh" or mouth in park!

Okay, folks, now that I have met Mister
Derek Jeter, All-Star Yankee shortstop
In person, shook his hand (has he kissed her?)
I can't holler Hey Butt-Man from the top
Row — it's not the same, I'm like a sister
Now (more like a mom). Protective. Tiptop.
He does have megawatt looks, upstaging
McCarver, who laughed at my rapt engaging.

Let's switch gears a bit here. I suppose you
Believe I've milked the Derek Jeter theme
For as much as it's worth (or more). His slew
Of charms are largely physical — tall, slim,
Delicate neck, broad shoulders. But vacu-
Ous, alas, alas. Not stupid! But seem-
Ingly not curious about poetry.
Is he interesting? Alas, not remotely.

One theory of crushes is that they must
Be adjacent decades: If you're in your
Thirties, you date twenties or forties. Just
Because he's cute doesn't sanction impure
Fascination for you-know-who — my lust

Is erased because he's so young. The lure
Less since in an interview he suggested
His future was business. Huh? He's bested

Most of the world in the money angle.
Why would he want to spend his life counting?
Jeter — like everyone — should want to wangle
Time for learning about himself, mounting
(No, not the ladies) the heights of tangled
Desires: revolution, poetry, pounding
Toward Parnassus. He'll have the leisure
Not to be dull, so why be a geezer?

Is it that it's easier when young to tear
Things down because you haven't actually built
Anything? The kids make me feel (unfair-
Ly) fuddy-duddy, when I see no guilt
(At times) defending bureaucracy. Spare
Me your absolutes. I'm pleased to the hilt
To pay taxes. As Adam Smith wrote, it
Means I'm not property myself. Noted.

Yesterday the All-Star game, invented by
My friend Beth's grandfather, in '33,
Arch Ward, who was a Chicago sports wri-
Ter. Beth had no interest in baseball — we
Hitchhiked, raged against the war and got high.
She was the first person I knew to be
Raised in an apartment, which I thought coarse,
Equal to divorce. Her parents were divorced.

I watched the first innings of the All-Star
Game, saw Jeter get two hits and score first
Run and predicted him MVP, far
Ahead of his third hit and AL burst
Of runs. Your boy is MVP, said Mar-
Vin, who works for my landlord downstairs. Versed
In my tastes — but someone I'd never spo-
Ken to before. How does everyone *know*?

III: PINK HIGHWAYS

Now it's time to shout "Allons! Come with me!"
As we hit the road, see the USA
By way of auto and thumb. My hobby
Is driving, but in an earlier day
It was my life. If invited, I'd be
Avid to split, or I'd spirit away
Alone. I had friends I was devoted
To all over the land, and I toted

Myself often to see them. No money
So I usually hitchhiked. I might veer
Off for weeks or months on a journey,
Or rumba a thousand miles in a mere
Weekend. Motion was all I wanted. Funny,
I don't feel that different now — to steer
With no output still seems the ideal life
Although these days I'm a worker and wife.

A few summers back I drove with Becky
From Eugene, Oregon, to the East Coast.
That is, with Becky and her two wacky
Springer spaniels, Emma and Jake. Foremost
Quality of springers is anarchy
Of attention and compliance. Milquetoast —
Not them. These dogs need to be tended to
All the time or it's a traveling zoo.

Springer spaniels are white dogs with brown, black
Or liver-hued patches and silky hair.
Excitable? Understatement! They lack
Decorum! Insanely friendly, with rare
Joy. We had to stop often, to unpack
Leashes, collars, dishes and let them tear
After birds. They're pointers, who spring straight up
Off the ground (hence the name), even as pups.

We're packing to leave Oregon. "Oh god
I hate change," Becky says with a deep sigh.
She's picking up quarters and nickels, dod-
Dering around her little house, so I
Am not certain which "change" she means. A nod
To the dogs. They leap in the car — they'd die
Rather than be left. And two "girls" alone —
We need these savage pups as chaperone.

Becky's traveling trick: "I'm taking all
My oldest underwear — the crappy stuff
That's stretched-out and unsightly and fall-
Ing apart, and every day I'll slough
It off." She flings her arms to show the sprawl-
Ing pleasure of America rebuff-
Ing her panties. We also like driving
For its inertia in the guise of moving,

And 'cause it's a daydream you can follow
To its end (assuming you're away long
Enough) and because we don't have to go
Over the Throgs Neck Bridge. I trust the throng
Of driving gods to get us home. My beau
Is a ton of real steel, singing and strong.
It pulls me like kids to a holiday.
I have no advice for the highway.

I love the highway for its industrial
Driving, its ramalamadingdong.
But the pink highways — the skinny radial
Roads — are pretty and soothing too, singsong
Easy driving. Many folks take parochial
Pride in staying off the freeway. Less headstrong,
I don't care, I like any road I'm on.
Never an ugly duckling, always a swan.

But now we're glad to be off the highway —
Also called freeway; in South Dakota,
Interstate; in Michigan, expressway.
Route 11 north to Walla Walla,
Washington. The cool thing here is that state

Road numbers are in George's head. What a
Great country, full of towns with such names as
Walla Walla, Pukwana and Ramses.

Me 'n' U Deli in Mapleton, OR.
Wild Winds, which I assumed was a peerless
Road sign. Nope, gated community, Flor-
Ence, OR. Autopia — I sigh in bliss.
Thistle Dew Antiques. The Pink Hole in Or-
Ofino. Fort Fizzle. Thrill-Ville U.S.-
A., an amusement park. InstaLawn
Back in Eugene: "We keep rollin' a lawn."

I was happy in Musselshell County
To indulge a hotel hobby — to "fix"
The art. On woodland scenes (firs and Mounties),
I draw dead dogs and peeing men, a mix
Of subjects that is easy (a bounty
For bad artists) and, I daydream, graphics
That may dissuade with my fiddle-faddle
The designs of someone suicidal.

In Montana, an older gentleman
With a springer fell for Beck. You're it, he
Cried, come be my bride, we'll live in my van
With our dogs. She declined. Though I could see
Why, I urged yes, with half a mind to can
Our trip: Imagine two hideously
Hyperactive kids in a small plane. *You'll*
Want to bail. One good point — these dogs don't drool.

In the old days you could hop on a plane
An hour after the thought occurred to you
To go somewhere; you didn't have to pay
Four times as much as those people who knew
Seven, fourteen, thirty days ahead that they
Intended a journey. One time I blew
Up Johnny's computer. In a panic
Decided to flee to Maine and Janet.

Fast taxi to LaGuardia airport.
Where I see an archetype from any
Year: A man pats himself down for his passport;
Some folks are reading, some sleeping; many
Eye the overhead TV. The sport
I've long relished of leaving town when e-
Vents grabbed me is booming. How great it is
To have planes like autos at my service.

I called Janet: "What's going on tonight?"
"The gang's in Hancock," she said, "otherwise
Just hanging out." "I'm on my way. It might
Be Bar Harbor — wherever the plane flies."
In an hour I was enroute, and that night
I partied. Sudden movement satisfies
The itch to subvert space-time, plus disengage
Mad husbands and other troubles of the age.

I used to fly under an assumed name —
Olivia Bennett, no, Jane Bennett.
Or was it Olivia Grey. The game
Of anonymity. Do I think it
Can be like that now? that maybe the same
Hitching imperative applies? One tenet
Of hitchhiking was to start off with a whiff
Of invention and continue to riff

On it till it was complex and detailed
By the time you got where you were going.
For instance, once, leaving Maine, I retailed
Info about my three kids, lies flowing
Effortlessly from me. I never failed
With an answer. I was secure, knowing
I could improvise. I was in love with
X— Y— then and based it on his three kids

(But only somewhat). I have learned from hitch-
Ing some principles. One: implicit trust
In my tongue. I can lie, and the words pitch
In and flourish. The trick is to get bust-
Ed in a fib (a good one) at times, which

Inclines people to suppose that you must
Be a bad liar. They've misunderstood
That all the rest of the time you *are* good.

Another rule that I took from my stretch
As a thumbmeister was to rely on
My intuitions of people. Was that lech
Ted Bundy? You had to see beyond
Looks. Guys made passes but a real wretch?
Nope. I never got in with anyone
Too skeezy. I made snap judgments and still
Decide right away about folks, and feel

I am rarely wrong. The new editor
At one mag — I knew straight off she was nuts
And vicious. Give her a chance, Elinor,
My colleagues said. You betcha, I said, but
Bided my time. In three weeks, plenty more
Knew what I did. That's one case of my guts
Working on my behalf. Maybe I turned
Down Ted Bundy for a lift! I'll never learn

The truth about my narrow escapes,
Which is the truth about life, isn't it?
The other fork in the road, those scrapes
You miss — you can't land in a different minute
Of the calendar. Any skipped landscape
Can only remain indeterminate.
That's why it is pointless to feel regret
(Except when you have hurt others). Forget

The road not taken and relish the grade
You're on. It is now the only option.
Hitching tends to make one mull, I'm afraid.
And that's something I expected to shun
In this poem. Philosophy might degrade
My limping brain. You think that won't wash? Un-
Theory is my middle name, and I cling
To my creed: Ideas aren't what make birds sing.

Beau one time referred to "the flow of life:
You're in it," he said. I *want* to be in it —
I want to be scraped by joy, fear and strife.
A lightning rod; peer of a peony,
The Chrysler building gleaming like a knife,
The smell of gasoline, the Leonid
Showers. They all are only what they are;
Meaning stuffed into beauty serves to mar

What's right in front of you: simple objects
But intricate too like the H4 clock
Devised by the winner of the project
To determine longitude. Weathercock
Didn't work. Latitude easy, this subject
Isn't, even though I read the book, chock-
Ful of explanations of time and tide,
None of which wedged too far into my hide.

In Helena, Montana, a salad
Was so perfect I vowed to move to this
Town. The "New York-style" deli less valid,
However. A forsaken town in wes-
Tern ND pulled Becky toward the pallid
Place in Georgia her dad came from. To miss
Where we have never lived comes from the power
Of landscape to invent memories not ours.

Why does one place land with full weight in our
Hearts while another jumps across our eyes
And is gone? Why recall some exploit, hour,
Incident or person? Is there a wise
Answer? Is it random, or does some power —
Say from childhood experience — give rise
To the varying import of what tumbles
Sticking or not, in the mind's jumble?

Being ardent fans of Ford Madox Ford,
Becky and I next made our obeisance
To Olivet College, Michigan, for
A stop at the Ford shrine, which indecent-
Ly isn't really there. This didn't floor

Us, knowing how overlooked he's been since
(And before) his death sixty years ago.
This English writer loved women and wrote

The mysterious yet scratchily open
Parade's End, my favorite, much re-read book
With sex-mad Sylvia ever-hoping
Christopher will sleep with her. But he took
Off with Valentine, saw England loping
Through billows of wild plants, World War I shook
Him up. He wants rest and a woman he
Can finish a talk with, quietly.

Here's another literary enthu-
Siasm of mine: Angela Thirkell,
British novelist of manners. Imbued
With class distinctions and wit, her circle
Of characters' complications ensue
From love and "subnormal" servants. A Turk'll
Acquire all she needs to know of prewar
England and its gentry's defective core,

Which are long since gone (or perhaps persist,
As despite change of circs, we still see Sloane
Rangers, e.g., and other class insist-
Ence). Her novels are delicate yet toned
With a clever eye that sees through the mist
Of relations, bad clothes and dimly known
Counties. She's relaxing to read, all her
Books the same. Trollope's literary daughter.

Becky hates RVs, as she says every
Time we end up behind one. I myself
Desire them desperately. Our treasury
For it was a water bottle of pelf,
Until Johnny learned what the nummary
Was for, dumped the change, broke the jar itself.
Becky thinks that shows what a sensible
Husband he is. Ha! Reprehensible.

My most loved car was a '73
LTD named Ford Madox Ford. Its flanks
Were painted blue, pink and green in cheesy
Latex housepaint, with magic marker'ed hanks
Of my poetry: "It will be easy
To drive away from this." Cops and cranks
Stopped me all the time: What inclinations
Led to "Dreams aimless as destinations"?

Another car I owned for years and cruised
90,000 miles was a Toyota Cor-
Olla. At length stolen; the cops refused
To look for a sixteen-year-old — on par
With searching for an old hat I might lose.
Poor little Yellow Bird, kidnapped and marred.
Well, her splendor wasn't exactly pristine.
She was too rusty to properly clean.

The fastest car I ever drove (versus
The car I drove fastest) must have been Paul
Stallings' Ferrari. Slowest? The worst is
My '70 Datsun 510, which qual-
Ified for many unkind curses
Each time it wobbled. Not a car to haul
Ass in! I loved it, though, as I did my
Every vehicle. Till we said goodbye.

For a year or so I owned a white Ford
Falcon van, '65, bought in Lansing.
We (my boyfriend, for the most part) ignored
That it had grave troubles. Got an engine
Off a Comet, a repair job nigh toward
Impossible yet we're soon advancing
To Maine in that wreck. The only unnamed
Car I ever possessed. It's not the same.

As with teams, a name implies relation,
And I do recall less about "the van"
Than of most of the cars in the nation
Of autos I've owned, though a few I can-
Not remember where I bought (a cessation

Of memory that bugs me). My mechan-
Ic sold Fordie, a Swiss guy owned Yellow
Bird, the Celica was Harris's, no

Other cars come to mind. Ernest we found
On the street, Sioux Falls. LeRoy the pickup
I dunno. The Merc came from the renowned
Sleazy Harry, Bangor. "Tell him — ayup —
Sandy sent you." Bad tranny and bad sound
From moving parts. By luck, the interrup-
Tion of theft before spending much for repair.
Cars come and go with love but not despair.

January 29's the birthday
Of the auto — first patent went to Benz
(Karl Friedrich) though many components lay
Waiting for assembly into sirens
That would lure many a speed freak to play
With dangerous beauty in asphalt gardens.
What's the allure of going flat-out fast?
To focus, to screech, to not be passed,

To keep breathing. What's exhilarating
Is having to be fully present, more
Than you think possible. You're not waiting
But in the thick of your senses and your
Talents, history, learning. And fading
Out is anything apart from your core.
My best work gets done that way, fully "on,"
Using my brain, wonderful, tiring, none

Of the usual distractions throwing sound
Tracks into the mix. Instead, it's as pure
As a mountain whoop. I put off the hound
Of inattention baying up what were
Foxy seductions. They did once abound
But now it is me alone with — inured
In — a shot propelled in one direction.
(These metaphors ebb with no objection!)

Here's a lot of tales from my bullet days:
Driving west on Route 2 through Maine with Pecos,
We stopped for a light in some podunk place.
A guy leaned out of a window (a ghost?).
"Come on up," he hollered out of a haze
Of pot smoke. "Come to our party!" Our host's
Father was there, a silent drunk. I was
Shocked. I had no idea that dads got buzzed.

On that drive we picked up a Canadian
Bum (not entertaining), went through Montreal,
Ate figs the whole way. What year? What radiant
Talk? Where I headed next I don't recall.
Pecos! With your heart-shaped birthmark! Custodian
Of thirty years of photos, waterfall
Of opinions and laughs, an alphabet
Of anecdotes, beliefs and few regrets.

Luck with money is an uncertain thing,
Unless you're rich already, in which case
You kick back for the ol' ka-ching;
Luck's not a factor there. Luck turns its face
To me so often I trust it to sing
When my ears are parched. I do have the grace
To wince at the mixed metaphor of that.
Don't hate me: Money drops into my lap.

A few years ago, when I was winding
Home from upstate New York, moseying back
Roads, I decided to stop at the Shrine
Of the North American Martyrs, quack
Attractions being great favorites of mine,
Though I didn't use to stop much; I lacked
An off toggle: Once in motion, I kept
Going, no matter what enticement leapt

Off signs begging me to visit. Water
Running uphill, mystery spots, a cave
Full of jewels. Even stops I oughter
Make, like presidential homesteads, I wave
At from my car. But the Shrine — the slaughter

Of priests "tomahawked for the faith," the brave
Mohawks, reminiscent of *Mangled Hands,*
Johnny Stanton's splendid novel — this lands

Me in Auriesville, which isn't a town
Just lots of giant Stations of the Cross.
Early autumn. I stroll the grounds, look down,
See a hundred-dollar bill. Is it poss-
Ible?! When I pick it up from the ground,
It's *nineteen* hundred dollar bills. Whose loss?
I waited twenty minutes for a hue
And cry. No one in sight. What would *you* do?

Standing alone on a road by a field
At daybreak, with the fresh grassy air
Rising in wisps, the sky turquoise and teal,
Cattle regarding you with solemn stare,
The top of your head about to yield
To its most feathery signal, where
You will yell and dance madly in the quiet
That is noisy, vehement with spring light.

Standing near an interstate overpass
In Iowa, on Christmas, in a blizzard
Cursing all the cars that zoomed by too fast
To notice me in what was a desert
Of white. I knew I would get home at last,
And I did, of course. As by a wizard,
That world was made small by whirling weather
And by knowing this couldn't last forever.

Squatting by a moonlit road in Vermont
To pee, my car silently rolled away,
Slowly, as if she were no more than saunt-
Ering a step or two toward the woods to say,
Hey, look at *this* pine tree, and then, her jaunt
Done, slide back. I let her go without dismay,
Didn't yank up my pants and leap at her.
The car rolled to a stop, as did my bladder.

Hitchhiking again after getting kicked
Off by the cops, then outraged that they came
Back: What?! Didn't they trust us?!? We were nicked
For thirty bucks each, me and Beth, a lame
Fine that we had to borrow from my ticked-
Off sister Lindsay. (Nah, from her no blame.)
An afternoon in the Dane County Jail
And that's all there is to that little tale —

Except to say we refused the baloney
Sandwiches. No one else was in the clink.
Beth and I tried out our best stony
Stares on the two matrons, who didn't blink,
No surprise: our looks were pretty phony.
I could see Madison's lake through a chink.
I knew Lindsay's cash would be effective
So couldn't feel myself truly captive.

A truck driver who played an eight-track tape
Of off-color jokes, over and over,
Without intentions. In Kansas, a scrape
With a drunk who stopped at every bar. *I* drove
Till my turnoff, parked the car, left him draped
Snoring in the back seat. A guy who loved
Paul Strand, excited to introduce me.
A woman with triplets in Missouri.

A guy with a scar and a '53
Chevy pickup who drove me five hundred
Miles out of his way. A six-piece country
Band and their bus in Georgia. The standard
Line of the many folks who offered me
Money: "Take a bus!" Truck drivers, wayward
Steel workers, farmers, whose intimate jive
Crept into the commonplace of our lives.

Hitching's not all just moments of standing
By the roadside, though that's when you feel most
Solitary, the entire sky landing
On you with a wide-awake crack; the host
Of wildflowers and a few undemanding

Cows or horses by a trough or fencepost.
You see clearest when you aren't where you are
Routinely. These pictures still feel so sharp.

Hitching has its advantages — low cost,
New faces — but a road trip in your own car
Is terrific also. You can take off
And pause when you want, select your route, part
Company with the freeway when you stop
Needing its smooth speed; and when you're too far
From an upcoming place to relax,
You jump back on the fast road and make tracks.

Computers are like cars — some people like
To drive, some hate it, most are indifferent,
Just want to get where they want to go. Strike
The band for technology! Ignorant
Driving leads to woes. But a motorbike
Or automobile can be operant
Without grasping how to fix the motor;
Okay to type knowing not one iota

About what makes a computer function.
If the owner has taken driver's ed,
Or computer ed in conjunction
With purchasing the contraption, then add-
Ing memory or spotting malfunctions
Are extra. At speed is fast enough. Dread
Makes us dim-witted. Hit every button,
I say. See what happens when you go on.

"See what happens" is not a bad approach
At that — something unexpected is bound
To turn up if you're watching. A cockroach,
For instance. (Not surprising in a town
Like New York.) The uncommon can encroach
The regular with a shift of profound
Or small consequence. A platitude here
Is called for, or maybe a glass of beer.

Whew — let's escape profundity (silly
Is more like it) with a bottle. A joint
More up my fireplace. I used to really
Smoke like a fish: I'd giggle, lose the point
Of conversations, and willy-nilly
Laugh, eat, leap up. Fun and then one day — boing! —
No more pot. I do love to reminisce
About the days when I had time like this

To be goofy, to do what came along,
Take off for months because somebody asked
Me and one move led onward. Being young
Was part of it. The '70s were a blast,
With plenty of us footloose. Nothing wrong
With having a good time. Motto: live fast
(But without dying young, if possible,
Including avoiding the hospital).

Driving around was something I could do
That was glamorous and didn't require
Me to have money or travel to Eu-
Rope, speak Swahili or even acquire
An education. It was what a screw-
Up could be good at (I can change a tire!
Do a brake job!) while keeping other skills
Out of sight of what seemed the world's perils.

Sometimes the past seems not gone but mislaid.
In dreams it is sometimes thirty years back,
When my hair was to my waist. Getting laid
And hitchhiking were the main things I stacked
My days with. I don't expect to evade
Whatever's next, but can't I once more pack
My knapsack, thumb to Maryland and see
Willis, Phil, J.D., Teresa, Billy?

It was many years ago today.
Beth and I hitchhiked down to Washington
D.C. for last-ever big demonstra-
Tion against the Vietnam war. Having fun
Was our plan more than expounding our vague

Politics. So it seems now. Being young
In '71 was a ball and who
Really knew what went on in the world? Who

Knew how complicated economics
And war are, how hard to find elegant,
Workable solutions. Without stomachs
To digest what was served, we became litigants
Demanding and expecting heroics
Sprung from shock and anguish. We yelled again
And again that the world — listen, my *dear*! —
Needs help and we are the only ones here.

Why do I keep getting away from
The prairie, the Great Plains, my native state,
South Dakota (I tend to say I come
From "the Dakotas")? I split, inchoate,
At eighteen, feeling stifled, bored, held mum
By what was still unclear, that art means trade,
Changing paint into paintings, words to poems.
Pre-artists often have interim

Restlessness and the idea to change
Themselves, not the material world; and think the road
To transforming oneself is to rearrange
One's location. Thus, despite SoDak's loads
Of potential, I felt only its chains.
So I left. Of course there are other goads
That turn people into artists, and we
Are likely to be spurred by two or three.

I didn't know I'd miss the prairie. It's June
In NYC and out west too, of course.
June is the plains' most pleasing month — soft noon,
Twilights long enough to surround the source
Of themselves and of all softness. This boon
Needed as the rest of the year is force
And bluster. I think I haven't drawn
A deep breath since my last Dakota dawn.

Even a New York City apartment
Morning can feel outdoorsy in June.
Some sort of bird, and the sough of the spent
Wind, which I may have translated from noon
Traffic. Squint past the fire escape to bent
Trees. My family was urban, the tune
Of our Nature muted and composed. Fine —
I prefer the country with city skyline.

I remember standing in our driveway
On the first day of summer vacation
When the gloriously promising days
Stretched ahead. The peonies' libation
Of scent and ants shook pinkly. A blue jay
Rattled in the pine I climbed impatient
For a view. The lilies of the valley
Next to the house, slightly off the alley

Would be gone by then — in spring I'd lie down
To drink their scent. I think no one else knew
They were there. Prairie sky above, a mound
Of cumulous clouds in billowing blue.
Plains are pure primary color, you drown
In floods of red, white, green and yellow, new
Every day, blown fresh by the eternal
Wind that swoops from vernal to infernal.

Sioux Falls — that prairie town, "heart of the Sioux
Empire," agricultural center *and!* my!
Birthplace! How autobiographical did you
Suppose I was gonna get here? Some prize!
What matters, what I'd like, is for you to
Appreciate the sheer beauty and size,
The waves of tallgrass, the rolling level
That's home to animals, plants — primeval

And contemporary — insects, Indians,
Ranchers, farmers and hard-assed cowboys
Like the ones I grew up with, guardians
Of stringent right-wing ideas. And choirboy
Swedes, the mostly silent Scandinavians

Who didn't laugh at the jokes I deployed.
That took moving east to New York, where a
Sense of humor is black as mascara.

My father was Hans, my mother is Joyce
My sisters are (the late) Edie, Lindsay
And Varda. A single brother (what rejoic-
Ing when the prince was born!) — that is Charlie.
Of the three of us close in age, I'm poised
In the middle, Vee is youngest by many
Years, and Edie was much older. Their tales
May show up again here (credit blackmail).

Besides a blood family, I have a twin,
O'Malley. Because of a shaggy dog
Joke I told that cracked Douglas up, he's been
Calling me that (and vice versa), in a bog
Of fake brogue. I've a "Mexican cousin"
And courtesy uncles and aunts. A fog
Of relationships. It's entertaining
And hopeful, and I'm really not feigning

These relationships. One's blood family
Is often more problematic, as they
Refuse to recognize the adult me,
Instead wafting anecdotes that replay
Adolescence, shooting a homily
Instead of listening. You're made to pay
Perpetually as the elder sister
Or the one who blubbered in a twister,

Of which SD has many. (A better
Subject than family.) On the other
Hand, kin's not just a matter of fetters:
You share the oldest jokes with your brother
And sis, the not-funny jokes that get her
Every time. That's how it works. Your mother
Can be discussed by people who regard
Her in the same way you do, who are hard-

Ly blind men and the elephant in this.
That terrible feeling of gaslighting
Can't work. You are being made crazy — if
You are — within yourself, not by fighting
Their attempt to push you in the abyss.
Is it true (who d'you suppose I'm citing
Here?) we are full of creatures and notions
That secretly control all our motions?

Another Becky-El stop: the Corn Palace
In Mitchell, SD. My favorite shopping
Spot — better than Bergdorf's! I am zealous
In scanning the a-maizing, eye-popping
Collection: pens shaped like corncob phallus,
Snow globes, caps, popcorn with many toppings,
T-shirts galore. All corn-themed. I love corn.
It's a central fetish since I was born.

Fields of corn along every road and rung.
I like how you see straight rows no matter
What angle you look at it; head-on, swung
Diagonal in perfect lines, ladders
Of satisfying symmetry. When young
I could distinguish corn with no natter.
Corn resembles itself from sprout to ear,
Unlike most other plants or trees or beer.

Corn is more like a friend in that regard,
Who doesn't disguise her voice when she phones,
Or wear wigs when you meet, to make it hard
To know it's her. Corn is itself, no bones
About it. I also like corn as the bard
Of prairiedise, the constant wind that moans
Through the fields, sings a duet with that grass
Spreading its generous heart like a gas.

Mountains are splendid but they offer too
Many views. The great thing about the prairie
Is that you're always in the middle; you
Always have the best vantage point. Airy
Grasslands soothe today as they did the Sioux,

64

Who completely understood how varied,
Useful and productive they are — perfect
Opposite of any alpine district.

Flat rivers of wild yellow mustard.
Rugosa roses, juniper, grama, yew,
Foxglove with its white, pink and custard-
Yellow bells. Magpies on markers. A slew
Of buttes, clover fields and beehives. Whiskered
Grain in a silo. It's my own land: true,
Familiar, flat and with the finest soil
In the universe, black and rich as oil.

Willa Cather's an old fave; I'm surprised
I hadn't read *Archbishop. O Pioneers*
Is the best plains book I've read. I advise
You to it. No one else makes it as clear:
The thrilling monotony, a sunrise
Like the dawn of the world, with all the years
Implicit in each day, so you relax,
Let yourself float into your life — sit back

Like Southerners, whose weather similarly
Lets them drift along. With no real seasons,
Nothing to wake you, sleep in the barley
Or corn, endlessly rocking. Malfeasance
Unlikely, watched by so much sky. Parley
Calm — Dakotans are known for their decenc-
Y. The four seasons here: winter, junction
To winter, still winter and construction.

Sioux Falls's a border town between the West
And the Midwest, and like all border towns
Not quite flesh nor fowl. Some swagger: biggest,
Farthest, but more typical are farm sounds:
Tractors creeping down a two-lane, the dest-
Iny to marry young and stay around.
Enough rain to farm in your granddad's dirt,
Knowing that a hundred miles west, the earth's

Arid, can't support more than runty wheat
And grazing — cows to eat rather than cows
For milk. Though speaking of cattle to eat,
Sioux Falls hosts huge stockyards. The whys and hows
Of meat-packing charmed a school tour, to eat
The proffered hot dog after — big ugh. Vows
Of vegetarianism shot like comets
Through us after a visit. And vomit.

"A whole lot of things I ain't never done,"
Sang Commander Cody (I do believe)
"But I ain't never had too much fun!"
Hitching rules: Don't ride with someone who weaves
Cross three lanes to stop for you. There's a ton
More advice: It doesn't matter how dev-
Ious, you can outwit them. The longer
The wait, the better the ride. Hunger

Is thwarted by taking every offer
Of food. Wash your face every chance you get.
(There is more, but as always, it's tougher
To absorb too much information.) Vets
Are the ones who really know; a duffer
Has to learn it all from scratch. Pay your debts.
If you want to learn, don't take 101 —
Always begin in the middle. I'm done!

I'm done — or perhaps I should amplify
Some of these remarks, or tell the stories
They're based on. In 1975
It was possible to get in lorries
Or cars, go off with strangers and defy
Warnings you heard all your life of gory
Outcomes. I don't these days travel the same
Way, so don't know if roads are wild or tame.

Old Route 66, Steinbeck's Mother Road,
Never drew me particularly — I
Pointed east, halfway to Europe. The code
Of the West was spoiled because I dwelt by
The West, a mere hundred miles east, no Joad

Was I, adventure's dramatis personae
Bored me. Yet deep in my American brain
The road falls steady and heavy as rain.

Today, though, I'm full of Route 66
("Chalk full," someone wrote me recently)
For readers with no desire or connex-
Ions to any road, how will I gently
Steer them to the magic, mystique and "kicks" —
A word used in *On the Road* plently,
Kerouac being inspiration and dad
Of all road trips. Or is he just a fad?

If so, he has been of cult devotion
For almost fifty years, subject of books,
Films, conferences, intense emotion,
Emulation — etcetera. His hook
Was going deep, fearless in the ocean
Of experience, so you knew if you took
To the road as he had, you'd meet the same
Gone cats, holy jazzmen and eager dames.

What was it that flung so many of us
Into such furious nonstop travel?
To drive, letting the road wind like Texas
Through us, took us out of the fierce battle
Of American life we despised. Hus-
Tling for bucks versus wanting what we have'll
Seem old news, but it was ardently fought.
I, for one, was resolved not to get caught

By conventional *anything*: job, marriage,
Home. The outcome: I live in a "starter"
Apartment (as some people disparage
It) and work freelance, not quite by barter
But no regular paycheck. A squarish
Relationship that's a little harder
To summarize in a line or two.
I love Johnny Stanton — will that do?

No, of course not. I'll have to explain the terms
Of how we go about our life together.
He'll hate this revealing. Shut up, El! He squirms
At my unprivacy. Oh well, he'll weather
This like so many other storms. He confirms
Storms but I can knock him down with a feather
Before he'll agree that we ever agree.
And that's marriage, kids, between Johnny and me.

Lounging behind the steering wheel with pave-
Ment flashing past under my tires settles
Me like nothing else. The car is my cave
Of existence, with nothing but pedals
And windshield in the world. If I could save
Focus this enormous for bills, my debt'll
Be at rest. Driving absorbs to the bone
Yet it also leaves you free and alone.

I learned that from my first car, a '50 Dodge
Schoolbus named Ernest. We did everything
In Ernest. Bought in South Dakota, lodged
In Denver, sold in Boulder. My next king
Of the road LeRoy, '54 Ford, hodge-
Podge of jury-rigged parts, in which we winged
It across the country — Colorado
To West coast and back East. The bravado

Of those days of driving through the wreckage
Of time and expectation, when we could
Take off for months with no slow-down baggage
About jobs, gardens and boyfriends. I would
Drive a thousand miles for a sweet message
Of friendship. If that sounds extreme, you should
Be aware that I grew up with a mom
Who drove hours for bagels without a qualm.

My father didn't drive at all, he stopped
The year I was born, because on a trip
To the cemetery, a passenger popped
Up in the back seat, prodded him and quipped,
"Hope this won't be a one-way journey." Pop

Pulled over, got out and never would nip
Behind a wheel again. I learned with no fuss
That women drive but men are too nervous.

Music mattered when you were cruising cross-
Country. The first song setting out — A.M.
Radio back then — set the tone. If the Boss,
Stones, Doors, Dylan or any song came
On with special significance, you would toss
Your past behind — you're on your way! To frame
The drive with totemic songs gave omens
Of adventure and bliss on your roamings.

Nowadays, what with tapedecks and CD
Players and a new sort of radio,
With satellite-sent songs coast-to-coast, to be
In cars soon — it's hard to recall the rodeo
Of music we took a chance on, greedy
For the new. You would holler "way to go!"
When good songs came on early in the drive:
A sign that this outing was gonna thrive.

Now no more portents, we're so in control,
We never hear a random song. Too bad.
Back then I'd whirl the dial for rock & roll,
These days I pop in Cash who's no less rad-
Ical than Dylan, with his hot-eyed soul
And working class allegiance. He stays mad
When he should. Too much rock music dances
Into self-love and fluttering trances.

To opera-loving Becky, Johnny Cash
Is a sore subject. I also listen to
Old country, R&B and blues, a hash
Of timbres and tempos, all of it mu-
Sic that drifts behind my focus — the flash
Of rock or Beethoven pulls me from du-
Ty. Good thing we barely have radio —
This car serener without stereo.

Some sights I like to see while on the road:
Highway architecture: the cloverleaves
Romanly rising overhead, an ode
To the massiveness of the land it heaves
Itself over. And the signs: I once towed
A road sign home, heavier than bequeathed
Money. They're the one thing American
That might outlast Disney and silicon.

When you drive round Italy, you see endur-
Ing chunks of Roman road and aqueduct.
I love to think people of the future
Will muse on the silos they see eruct-
Ating from the prairie, architecture
Imposing, while they wonder if it sucked
To live in the olden days. How entranced
They'll be that we pictured ourselves advanced.

Rather than trash our neighbors, let us turn
Toward (or, on) Midwesterners. I am one
Myself, so this will have a nasty kern-
El of self-appraisal. Am I a Mon-
Day morning New Yorker now? Do I spurn
My roots or embrace what I chose to run
From way-back-when? I'm neither queen nor ace,
Fish nor fowl. I can't be from the one place

I'm really from and I will never quite
Be from New York, no matter that I've lived
In Manhattan half my life, a sight
Longer than SoDak. How can I divvy
Up my attention or love, how indict
One by preferring the other, or stiff
One by tipping my heart elsewhere? I can't
Choose — I'll always be some sort of transplant.

IV. ALMOST CHOSEN

1.

Just so you don't think I can only write
About me, let's switch subjects for a bit
(I'll be brief here, kiddies, so hang on tight)
To, okay, let's see, Beckett or Smollet —
Is there trouble on those fronts? Human rights
In Sudan — that is important! Don't hit
Me for this skimpy attempt. I will come
On my next pass a bit closer to home.

Something that truly concerns me, no joke,
Is — aw, it sounds so solemn just to leap
To a pronouncement — solemn and hokey.
I'm an active volunteer with a heap
Of groups. In the summer I work with folk
Who watch trees in Tompkins Square Park to keep
Them free of Dutch elm disease. My single
Outdoors endeavor. I like to mingle

With those who live or hang out in the park.
"Whatchoo looking for," they ask when they spot
My binoculars. Pigeons, I might bark.
I can't see well and am never sure I've caught
The signs of sickness. It's no less a lark
To be out of a summer morning, not
Something I remember to do enough.
Claustrophiliacs find nature too tough.

Ben and I strolled in Tompkins Square one night.
I measured all the trees around their — "girth,"
He supplied. Strange ritual: at a height
Of four feet, wrap tree with tape measure (mirth
At tree-hugging pothead myth). Point: to cite
Tree growth. Ben lives in the woods, on the earth,
More than indoorsy me — but perhaps no tree
Matters to him as to the Conservancy

For the East Village Parks, where each tree lands
Like a newborn panda, coddled, its growth
Watched. The ratio of trees to people stands
Opposite here as upstate, I'd say. Both
Abundant in their own spheres, with garlands
And gangs plentiful as needed, the slowth
Of trees here and folks there akin, in fact,
And each of us prefers it where we're at.

I've tutored and mentored and coached Little
League (boys, but frequently one girl would play;
She'd often be the best, due to drilled skills,
Early growth spurt and stubbornness). I'm a
PEN prison mentor. I tithe for goodwill:
The best money is what you give away.
I'm on boards of two nonprofit unions.
Best of all, I'm free with my opinions!

I do a lot, too, at my synagogue —
Usher captain, visit the elderly,
Whate'er rabbi asks from the catalogue
Of shul urgencies. Sleep-deprived, surly,
I don't this a.m. feel do-goody, fog
Of hormones, hate (anxiety) — surely
You know by now I get carried away;
Poetic license comes with hell to pay.

Years back, I fell in with some Orthodox
Jews from darkest Brooklyn, where they raise strict
Technocrats, who disapprove of non-lox-
Eating me. I learned to dress in restrict-
Ed fashion — floor-length skirt, long sleeves, boxy
Shoes, and to likewise severely constrict
Gossip, a no-no that in its absence
Made me feel safe in Boro Park, "passing."

I worked in a store that sold religious
Books and items. Store life was chaotic,
Crammed with pious quarrels and prodigious
Studying. When I expressed quixotic
Attraction for the verve and litigious

72

Energy, Johnny said, "More exotic
To many people than a Brooklyn Jew
Is one who's from South Dakota, like you."

Ah, Judaism is a foreign country
(Perhaps all religions are) with its own
Language, customs, demands and pageantry.
You may be misled because much is known —
People who live there are your ancestry
And your friends, but believe me, it's home on-
Ly to natives; those who are émigrés
Stick out in subtle but definite ways.

In the Bible a most instructive tale
(Judges 12:6) is that of Shibboleth,
A word that pushed Ephraimites, when they failed
To pronounce it properly, to their death.
We may no longer kill when one can't nail
The word, but we judge harshly nonetheleth.
I've been told I'm not a real Jew because
I come from South Dakota and no Jew does.

A nice, well-brought-up girl from the Midwest,
That's me! Friendly, polite, well-mannered,
I give directions cheerfully to guests,
Who say New Yorkers are unlike they're bannered
To be, that is, rude — no, they're in fact blessed.
They don't know that natives tend to be inert.
New York's energy comes from immigrants;
It's as much Minnesotan as incumbents.

The same way that the Dead Dogs were the fringe
Of baseball but the real deal nonetheless,
The Nauens were weirdly Jewish, yet I challenge
Anyone to say we were any less
Valid than a rabbi or to impinge
On our self-definition with assess-
Ments that reject us from their narrow slot.
Jews come only from New York? Tommyrot!

What was I, in later life a Jewish
New Yorker, *doing* in South Dakota?
Not the typical Norwegian who is
A farmer, my dad came with a coat, a
Trunk and not much more. We were distinguished
As Jewish, though I've more than an iota
Of Lutheran in my nature. Resultant:
One Jewish-American Protestant.

How being a SoDak Jew differs from
NY: Our rabbi didn't have a bar
Mitzvah. No services were held in sum-
Mer. For that matter, no Saturday ser-
Vices; Friday ran twenty minutes. Come
Late, you'd miss it. I didn't know how far
We were from strict, as I didn't know what a
Hick I was till I left South Dakota.

It *was* close to being a Protestant —
Genteel, with lots of responsive reading
Rather than going one's own pace; distant
Not loud and embracing. Organ. Heeding
The fact that Reform sprang from a persistent
Desire to assimilate, this ceding
No big surprise. It's stressed more in a small
Community, magnified like my drawl

When I cross the Mason-Dixon line,
Embarrassing my genuine Southern
Friends. In Brooklyn's Boro Park, where nine-
Tenths of the people live by the lantern
Of Torah, one cannot help but define
Oneself in terms of Judaism, strengthened
In this by the very air being Jewish.
Where I'm from, a Jew is only Jew-ish.

When my bro was in law school, he confect-
Ed a seder — the Passover buffet —
For the SoDak prison. At the prospect
Of getting steak, the Jewish popula-
Tion of the prison trebled. Why correct

74

Their distortion? It led to a bouquet
Of marriage proposals. (The announced "steak"
Inedible. A mistake to partake.)

I'd say mine was a Jewish education
And upbringing, but not the Jewish life —
Kugel, cholent and Catskills vacation —
Known as (a word new to me) Yiddishkeit.
In New York, culture has little relation
To religion for most Jews. The light
Of Torah shines from Woody Allen's eyes
Rather than the teachings of the rabbis.

"Shabbat, Shabbat ... yadadadadada yadadada
    "Shabbat, Shabbat ... yadadadadada yadadada
        "Every time I go to shul
        "Something is on my mind ...
        "If you do what God wants you to
        "Baby, you'll be divine.
    "Shabbat, Shabbat ... yadadadadada yadadada
        "Shabbat, Shabbat ... yadadadadada yadadada."

Johnny made this up and sings in a croon
Reminiscent of the '50s — Elvis
Meets Dean Martin, complete with a platoon
Of snapping fingers and head dips. No malice
To it — it's a love song, in fact. I swoon
When he sings it to me, his careless
Charm and his pleasure in delighting me
One more thread in our marriage tapestry.

Would I stand and be counted in a crack-
Down? Would I be a hero or would I
Act as if I don't see and turn my back
On those who need help? Like a Luddite
Who opts out of motorized life, a pack
Is made of moral Luddites. Asked: "Should I
Be good?" they turn to medieval morals
And rest on their antiquated laurels —

Saying, "I gave a shiny nickel
And that discharges my obligation."
With the world in such an awful pickle,
We can't act like such a distant nation,
As though to be a hero is fickle
And in the past. Alas, no vacation
From duty is given us — think of AIDS,
Starvation, war, suicide bombs, crusades.

From Johnny a whiff of "holier than thou"
For even mentioning my interest
In Judaism, so I hesitate — how
Can we thrash this subject out in the best,
Least off-putting way. I suddenly now
Hear Dantean echoes in this theme, this quest
Toward a spiritual life. And know full well
Dante cowered before he entered Hell.

I guess it never really feels like I'll
Run out of time. I'm still getting started!
If not right now, then down the road, I'll dial
The guilt-o-meter and fix things. Darted
Off to pleasures and speculation while
I should concentrate. I won't be parted
That easily from my flaws. If it's Yom
Kippur every day, what is there but doom?

I bother more about people than God.
I think God is okay with that. How you
Treat human beings counts more. I'm not dod-
Ging God but thinking over how to
Live. "Inner peace, outer obnoxious." Mod-
Ern folks may reject this but that's not Jews.
The usual route of guilt/repentance/
Forgiveness lies not in words but events.

White shutter, red curtain, geranium.
The glamour is for France, not these homely
Objets. The bread here is my manium —
It's cheap, abundant, crusty and comely,
Crisp and soft as it swoops into my cranium

Then moves on down. I could wish my home be
Quiet in its bliss and anguish of living,
Not get louder than the joys of heaven.

Will I ever not be sad in Paris?
I try to grasp that it's a spiritual
Sin to be sad, as being querulous
Means avoiding joy. Also, habitual
Gloom is conceited: "*I'm* the most various
Sinner." Or so I understand the ritual
Requirement to rejoice, from Chassidic
Texts my rabbi quoted. Will I heed it?

How can I care so much and also be
Indifferent? Is it like passing out when
You have way too much work, when being slee-
Py is a way to be anxious? I can
Live without — that's my mantra, sort of. De-
Pressed-sounding, innit? But if you know men
(Humans) only leave and die, you are prepared
To cope with the inevitable merde

Of their disappearance. I no longer
Expect weird breakups with my friends. My friends
Are permanent now, unless they wander
Into the valley of (say it, El) death,
Where the shadows reach across to conga
Me enticingly. To rest. That thought sends
Warmth to envelop me shawl-like, shroud-esque
But if the heat comes on in the Pound, I'll pass.

Interlude

Is raining?
Yes, is raining.
Is raining hard?
Yes, is raining hard.
—Maggie Dubris

In '71 I lived for a while
In Severn, Maryland, a mile from Fort
Meade, where the Air Farce had a presence. Riled
By the war, Beth and I hitched to support
A gigantic antiwar demo, mile
Upon mile of vehemence and exhort-
Ation. There she met a GI named Wayne,
An easy-going airman who had lain

Next to her on the Mall. They woke up, smiled
At each other and were inseparable
For the next three years. Wayne, as a cook, wiled
Away his service in memorable
Fashion, amassing grievances, a pile
We admired as proving he kept the bull
Of war conformity out of his herd.
Wayne's in Alaska now from what I've heard.

That same day I met Steve, Sam, Wayne and oh,
Man, who was the fourth man? This ancient lore
Runs so deep, I can't believe I don't know.
Was it Billy? I'm sure it wasn't For-
Rister. Oh, of course! Phil. And that's the low
Down on the original gang. Air Force
Men, from small towns mostly in the Midwest
Or South. Their dads served in the War and stressed

Patriotism and traditional
(*Not* Republican) values. They believed
In America the Good, the mission of
Our men to proclaim liberty and bleed
For the cause. I can't mock. Additional

78

Evidence notwithstanding, of crimes heaved
Upon the world by our wars, they were stressed
Ever after, paid the price for our quest.

"Irritable heart" — the Civil War name.
"Railway spine" came up for train accident
Survivors. "Soldier's heart" (World War I), blame
Squarely on battle. Also "shellshock," faint
And nerves following clamor. The next claim —
"Battle fatigue" (World War II). Incidents
Of severe anxiety, dazed manner,
Exaggerated startle. The banner

For this today, and the least poetic
Moniker of all, is that accepted
Into the psych manual: "post-traumatic
Stress disorder." You'll find they have kept it
And once more, the evocativatic
Word is abandoned for the tepid.
Still and still. To every age, we keep
Doing harm, and deep still calls to deep.

«« — »»

To the north, a fall sky of bluest blue,
Chrysler Building bright as a dragonfly
In the September sun. To the north, you
Can see the city undiminished by
Collapse or terror. What's been added: new
Fears, chemical and human ash, the cry-
Ing of the falling, who are both the ones
Who perished and us, whose lives are a lunge

To escape a date that is nonetheless
Someone's birthday or anniversary.
Three weeks later, fires still burn in the mess.
Sixteen acres of jagged steel, nursery
For nightmares and uncertainties. The res-
Cue workers go on in the cursory
Manner of the starved, stripped of any plan
But to trudge toward a place where a man

Can scratch out a bit of corn from the earth
Or even find a body part that shows
That we once lived in this city and worked
High above it. To discover what blows
We can take after we navigate birth
And our own nature. Once politics slows
Our hearts, generosity and wonder
Shift from automatic and are sundered.

How can one feel as much for The Other
As for one's own? Humanity requires
It, yet our hearts might have room for brother,
Sister, nephew, niece and parents. What choirs
Of pleas can tempt us to embrace another
With full heart? Even God no doubt desires
This sparrow over that one, giving it
The gifts of safety, music and orbit.

My bouncy Midwestern optimism
Has begun to bubble like antacid,
Neutralizing the dark pessimism
I've been feeling ever since the massive
Attacks of 9/11. That barbarism
Means that I can no longer be placid
And go about my cheerful life of cars
And baseball. We must prepare for the dark.

Ben and I walked Broadway to Ground Zero,
Two weeks after the attacks. It's Broadway,
But rearranged. Here cordoned off, there o-
Pen to gawkers who stare then tramp on, flayed,
As far as they can go from the heroes
Who, though exhausted, continue their day
Of shoveling rubble, hoping (hoping!)
To find a finger, bone or purse. Hoping.

I climbed up on my roof and saw the world
Aflame, the World Trade Center with a bulge
Of fire, the white city orange, a whirl-
Wind of dirty smoke, heavy with divulged
Lives turned inside out, files and bodies hurled

From past to a present where to indulge
In the future is a luxury no
Longer routine. What's left: To worry low

And long about bioterror, atom
Bombs and recessions. And psychic damage —
Losing faith in order, where we had 'em
By the tail, where we'd throw on pajamas
And sleep through the night, where a platinum
Ring doesn't melt, assassins don't rampage
At will, people are left alone to dream
Through their years, and the world is as it seems

And seldom the sound of sobbing. Anthrax
The latest scare. Once a disease of wool
Sorters, sending its microbes by mail smacks
Of biowarfare. Journalists are full
Of themselves as targets. Adirondacks
Are starting to exert a stronger pull.
What kind of people aim at innocents
And wish to die to accomplish vengeance?

These days it's as though all of us in New
York have been holding our breath, and now we're
Passing out. I am listless, done in, blue.
It's like shaking hands with an amputee.
We may believe there's been contact, but few
Of us can throw ourselves with beauty
Intact into the arms of those we love.
At best we touch from afar, wearing gloves.

The folks who are sick of talking about
It versus those who're still obsessed. Each side
Leery of the other. "It's time for stout-
Hearted souls to buck up." "We must abide
In sorrow." What's more tentative are doubts
About feelings rather than deeds. A guide
Through terrorism and Afghanistan
Would be helpful. Where o where is Wystan?

It's stupid to put a real, ongoing
War into ottava rima, but e-
Qually inane to think about crowing
Over any heartening little de-
Tails of my day or life. When three Boeing
737s slam into three
Buildings, on purpose, the world has warped
In glancing blows that hit and aren't absorbed.

Art must persist, in the face of cockeye
Catastrophe. Auden later rejected
His poem "September 1939"
With the line we've all been affected
By: "We must love one another or die."
It's rushed to have the dreadnoughts selected
As a "low dishonest decade," although
Better might be "reaping what we sow."

"The best lack all conviction and the worst
Are full of passionate intensity."
The good poets right now despair of poems nursed
By the bombings, while the propensity
Of the lame is to flutter into verse
With poems that address the immensity
Of their darling feelings. I'm angry at
Everyone — bad artists, the Left, my cat.

Six weeks on and the air still so awful
That everyone is sick, slow and cranky.
If I didn't poke him, would my lawful
Husband ever kiss me? Hanky-panky
Ever ensue if I didn't boff him,
Or, that is, propose it? Would the Yankees
Play better if I were getting laid more?
Would the sky be bluer if they would score?

How come we know the names of the demons,
Not their victims? Mengele and McVeigh
But not the Levys, Cohens and Niemans.
I heard an Oklahoma victim say
"He got his" with satisfied vehemence,

And thought, McVeigh can't be made to pay
Even though you kill him. That's the problem
With revenge: It doesn't work. Hobble him

Or stare him in the eye, he won't see you.
The deaf are deaf however much you shout.
Do I need transitions to quote to you
The French actress Arletty's fabled flout?
Accused of treason for a boyfriend who
Was German, she defiantly spouted
This reply: France owns my heart's passional
But my pussy is international.

It's difficult to care for Zanzibar.
"The death of one man is a tragedy,"
Stalin said; "the deaths of a million are
A statistic." Our world is a CD
We can play whenever we want, discard
When we want, also. I'm a gadget, see?
A mechanical response, a reflex.
Elephants don't feel the fleas on their necks.

Shomrim are "watchers." A body is not
To be left alone until it's buried.
Shomrim (sometimes for pay) stay on the spot
Reading psalms* till the funeral's carried
Out. It's what one can do without a lot
Of money or learning. So I queried
A man who arranged a shomrim project
At the Trade Center morgue. The theologic

---

* XXIII
Sire is mi shepe • namore I shal suffre.
He ladde me on the mead • or by the marsh.
He shryuen mi soul, • gyed me streyte
Saustne of Hir stede. • Yea, tho I sueth depe Dale o Ded
I fere no fende. • He me folwe.
His steyke an His staf • hem me solace.
He prouendeth me myd payn • bifor piloures;
He assoilen me myd gris; • mi cuppe brimme ouer.
Sykerly goode an grace • shall myd me go
Alle mi lief-long lyf • An lodgen me
In Heuenriche forevre.
            —translated into Middle English by Elinor Nauen

Issues are few, always a bonus for
Those of us with little agility
To follow intricate reasoning more
Than a flash. My mental ability
Needs a beginner's seminar in or-
Der to function. A small facility
Can be enough for spiritual growing.
My main talent in life is for showing

Up, which I do at the morgue for an hour,
A couple times a week. Is it enough?
There's always one moment when the power
Of praise and rebuke hits me, when the stuff
Of armies and my own lacks are devoured
By joy and thanks. It's often just a puff
Or two of genuine human response
But it calms and woos me for the nonce.

Months and years later, people's sad stories
Are still being told. I'm back to "normal,"
But it can't be with the easy glories
Of pre-9/11, when hormonal
Change was all I dreaded, rather than gory
Reality. I try to be formal
But drawing sharp borders doesn't contain
My dreams, imagination or my pain.

2.

I dreamed I had to shave off my moustache.
It was like wrestling a roach — a slithery
Thing of wiry legs that I had to bash
Down. Meaning? Some disfiguring misery,
Overused habit that I now must slash
From my life? It makes me feel jittery
Because, I guess, I'm comfortably immured
In a life that includes this ugly beard.

A couple of blackguards sitting around
Talking — plotting — really just me and my
Bad character. Once more, my sins abound
In fall, what with the holidays, crying
For my lacks and acts. All of this is crowned
By my stubborn unwillingness to try
To become a better person. Why change
When one's quirks fall in the "delightful" range?

As I once read somewhere, what we call faults
At twenty-five transmute into pleasant
Idiosyncrasies when we are fort-
Y. Stubborn? No, *principled.* Hesitant
To even see, let alone try to halt,
Our bad traits. Accept, yes, but that doesn't
Mean they are not destructive nonetheless
And worth the struggle — even with small success.

If someone tells me that they go to church
Every day, I assume they're a nut.
I go to shul every day, but perch
So precariously on belief as to cut
Logic and faith to bits. I guess I'm "search-
Ing," and I do like the rituals, but
I'm so dismayed by inconsistency
That I'm contemplating delinquency.

Every day I walk up to Fourteenth Street
At seven a.m. for morning service
And think, Why am I doing this? What feat
Of juggling has made me impervious

85

To the contradictions of an upbeat,
Enlightened gal mixing with a nervous
Ancient religion? Is it making me
Better to be in a shul with my plea?

Johnny thinks so — "nicer" was his word choice.
I guess I'm not really sure what the goal
Even is, since I can't seem to endorse
A stance on the presence of God or soul.
I've resolved to assign whatever force
Is the reason for existence the role
And name "God." It's how to live in the presence
Of the mystery that tests my essence.

Ennui or accidie was once a sin
And now an aspiration. Those who are
Melancholy look down on the cheerful in
Their "shallowness." Yet despair is not far
From forfeit. Why do people seem proud to hin-
Der good works and choose futility? Hard
As it may be to believe the world works
Well, it's worse to live where hopelessness lurks.

For many, involvement in religion
Is for community, having a gang
Of like-minded comrades. Any smidgen
Of theology is *so* not the shebang
They concentrate on. A flock of pigeons
Likes a cozy huddle. Getting to hang
Together obviates the need to think
Alone, but alas, alone do we sink.

I've quipped that the folks at my synagogue
Have good characters, bad personalities,
While the poets, in the justifying fog
Of their art, have good personalities
And bad characters. Language seems to hog
The moral high ground where realities
Of ethics loom — but for others. Where do
I fall? The worst of both, I guess. And you?

How thoughtful to put on a low-cut shirt
When I go to the nursing home. Irving
Likely gets little chance to have to dowse
Any fires caused by a glimpse of curving
Female flesh. Although old ain't dead, no spouse
Is left to light those fires. I am serving
His manhood with this sexy dress. What harm
In giving old men a hint of my charms?

Why of eight hundred rules do you follow
These? Johnny has asked. What's this Jewish thing
Of yours? One day a week I don't wallow
In the things of the world — I leave off writing,
Driving, handling money, using the phone, go-
Ing to movies. Does he think I'm doing
It to irritate? as disapproval
Of his practice? A spouse's removal

From politeness is deemed normal. The wall
Of Torah-thumping to repel, censure
Or as goad to convert? He doesn't haul
Grudge, although marital dementia
Can be to see everything as cabal.
He's cut out most needling but adventure
Never looks quite the same to a husband
Who against whimsy has long since hardened.

It's not eight hundred, but six-thirteen
Commandments (or *mitzvot),** many of which
Involve Temple worship and so have been
Dumped. Many *mitzvot* exist in the niche
Of common sense — no murder, say. "Unclean"
Animals can't be eaten: Those laws are to ditch
Or adhere to not because they make sense
Or in expectation of recompense

---

* I now have my own set of tefillin,
The boxes that Jewish worshippers strap
On when they pray. Not sure yet I'm willing
To wear them every day. The gender gap?
Traditionally, they're for men. No villain
Forbids me but women aren't on the map,
Pretty much. (Not that that's ever stopped me.
Being told No tends to root me like a tree.)

But because, as the rabbis clarify,
God wants it that way, in order to make
Us realize the world doesn't signify
In rational, obvious, easy takes.
We may look for reasons to qualify
These laws as logical but that's a mistake.
We do them to direct our attitude
To commitment, duty and gratitude.

One topic that perplexes me is prayer.
I pray a lot — I'm in the synagogue
Most every day. What is it good for? Where
Do my prayers go? I'm often in a fog
Of lilting thoughts. Attentiveness is rare —
It's tough for me to ask or praise without bog-
Ging down in second-guessing. It's okay
To not be skilled. I do it anyway.

In fact, a big portion of what I like
At shul is my spiritual non-talent.
I am humbled by my ungainly hike
Through its rituals and claims. I have no bent —
But there I am. Once no longer a tyke,
We tend to stick with what we're proficient
At — I no longer cobble (see my scars?).
Garden (dead, dead, dead) or hang out in bars.

What does it mean that each and every day,
I repeat the exact same prayers and psalms,
In the exact same order, and find they
At times hit me upside the head like bombs?
Boom! Pay attention! I guess you could say
It means they're fresh, or it might mean the qualms
Of inattention or stupidity —
Can't I learn a thing with rapidity?!

There's a line in Psalm 118 I like:
"Open the gates of righteousness." I read
A gloss that said it means the righteous strike
The ground low every day, hoping to head
Directly into prayer, and as pikers,

As it were. I always feel the imped-
Iment of tyrohood; reading that made
Anxiety about aptitude fade.

Eight days a week is not enough to show
My love, said God, that's why I created
Chanukkah and Passover, all the slow
Holidays; surely you will be sated
By scads of feasts, extra psalms, joy in mo-
Tion of obligation and old custom.
New Year's and the Day of Atonement too,
When the shofar should rouse and center you.

The shofar is the most simple and old
Musical instrument, merely the horn
Of a goat or sheep. Because of the Golden
Calf, it can't be from a bull. A forlorn
Sound ... war cry ... triumph — there's a lot more rolled
Up in blowing than you might think. Though born
To play violin, I switched to shofar
And blew all over town this year. (Sho far

Sho good.) I blew like I was trying to throw
A baseball hard enough that it would leave
Earth's trajectory. I wanted to go
Blasting to heaven. An alarm to cleave
And a plea for mercy. I felt as though
I were a fountain with the prayers we've
Prayed balanced aloft in the noisy spume,
With leniency sent in place of doom.

I love Passover but never feel ready.
This year was typical — I cleaned one shelf
Two weeks ahead, ate up all the bread,
Shopped a bit, tried to examine myself
For inner leavening, i.e., pride. Fred
Brought me kosher toothpaste. With an elf
I could do much more. I'd hoped for a strike
From Johnny's union, so he'd dam the dike

Of errands, errands, errands that cascade
So darn incessantly into my life
That it's all I can do to barricade
With an iron to-do list. I need a wife!
Someone to get stamps and food, serenade
My endless correspondents, take a knife
To the clutter. And then comes a day when
I can forget my weekday acumen.

That is Shabbat — the crown jewel of the week.
I have almost no mixed feelings about
My Saturdays, when I get time to seek
Peace and do no work — don't write, drive or pout,
Refrain from cooking and sorrow. Unique
In the world three thousand years back, no doubt.
As Johnny's quoted, the Jews invented
Weekends. Shabbat reminds us we've rented

And don't own our lives — it makes me humble
And grateful. This is surely a message
I need to hear frequently, let rumble
Through my life, trying to let the knowledge
Work into me without such a jumble
Of evil aim and personal wreckage
As often spins us from what we intend
(The Good) to a compromising backbend.

Friday night is the best part of Sabbath
(All Jewish holidays run from sundown
To sundown). We sing psalms in the most splendid
Melodies imaginable. At Town
And Village, my home synagogue, people
Are overjoyed to be there for the shutdown
Of the evening, bow in the Sabbath bride
Who's also queen, inviting her inside.

All kingdoms of anger dissolve now, says
The mystic Zohar; each Jew is given
A fresh new soul for the Sabbath day's
Enhancement. The day's a piece of heaven
Or eternity, it's time out of space.

The metaphors are lovely and moving,
Inspiring, though I don't necessarily
Get the meaning behind them (or barely).

No matter how bored I may get in not
Working on Sabbath, I treasure and claim
That day of rest. Sometimes Shabbat has got
A positive fix, where I near the aim
Of holy connection, not read a lot
Of junk, yak with my sister or play games
On the computer. That's the goal, of course —
To steer toward God, not just avoid the coarse.

They say the Torah was written in black
Fire on white fire. It's the Jews' living book,
Our way, our conductor. It burns in back
And in front, a guide, a presence, a noodge.
The eyes of deep believers show no lack —
Torah is all. Or can be if you look
For it with open heart and willing mind.
Yes, mind is required too for Jews, you'll find.

A vital part of my interest is learning
To read Hebrew, beyond the rudiment-
Ary. I don't grasp it well yet, yearning
To both comprehend and to be fluent.
If this is the language that in burning
Letters created our environment,
I must master it. I'm partway along —
Stumbling but not always entirely wrong.

Come sing with me! Or, you may not want to.
Why would you think my voice has any "whew!"?
Or that the song I've picked from a fondue
Of creamy candidates has any ooh
Lah la? Or's in English. My rendezvous
With rhapsody is, in fact, in Hebrew.
To put it clearly, I'm learning to chant
Torah with its proper music and slant.

My head is filled with Torah trop, the trills
Waxing as background to all endeavors.
(I suppress them in the bathroom.) The thrills
Of reading Torah: first off, I never
Expected to sing in public, which fills
Me with surprising performance pleasure.
But it's not so much my own role really
As the holy Hebrew rolling through me.

I am fascinated with every step
Of learning — staggering through the Hebrew,
Trying out the notes, finding a way to schlep
To the correct interval, tracking Hugh,
My teacher, in rote but entrancing rep-
Etition of basic patterns, learning new
Tricks and subtleties as in any art,
Where as an insider, you're set apart.

You can't touch the parchment it's written on
With your bare hand. Black fire on white fire.
If you are a member of lit-anon
Trying not to read in such quick-gulp piles,
You'll find with Torah you have bitten off
Less and chewed more, gone deeper and higher
When you learn one short passage very well,
Slowed down instead of racing through pell-mell.

I slowed down enough last year to observe
A bat mitzvah, a coming-of-age rite
I missed back when I was thirteen. I'd swerved
In my studies but when the time was bright
To commit myself, I summoned my nerve
And stepped on the ladder of law and right.
To scan Torah then set it on a shelf
Wasn't enough — I had to try it myself.

«—»

92

Of the world's religions, which have fewest
Adherents? From most to least, I'm pretty sure
It's Christians, Muslims, Hindus, Buddhists, Jews.
It's hard to be Jewish. Persecuted
Widely in the outside world, and with slews
Of stiff obligations to execute
From within. But I *am* a Jew and seem
To need to be what I'm anyway deemed.

"Forsaking trust, the Middle East hurtles
Backward," says today's Sunday *Times* headline.
In one psychology test, a circle
Of folks surrounds you; you fall as a sign
That you trust them to catch you. Fertile
Metaphor, Fertile Crescent, and you can whine
That you were cast out if they catch someone
But you. What counts is how the story's spun.

And of course here's exactly how it turned
Out. Everyone feels betrayed by history, which
Keeps such thick clouds of expectation churned
Around each move that it's a grueling sit-
Uation to resolve. They feel burned
By media, UN, leaders; any hitch
Seems a stab in the back. So a place of holy
History is being exhausted, slowly.

Have I suffered? Or gotten off easy?
Oh sure, I've suffered, but I mean, have I
Been burdened? People can be cheesy —
My life's not just a cracked fingernail, right?
But competitive suffering — ugh, queasy-
Making. I'm still not saying this right. Why?
Have I suffered enough to feel as bad
As I do? Is that the right question, Dad?

Daddy managed to get out of Nazi
Germany a step ahead of the war:
January of '39. That's i-
Ncredibly close and instead of more
Family behind, he was first (foxy)

To get out — but last too. He had a vor-
Acious need to close this off from his kids.
But secrets can leave those outside wretched.

It all goes back to my father, I'm told.
His losses — family, language, country,
Which he locked away from us. Can I be bold
Enough to drag it out? But why? If I'm free
Of pain does it put me out in the cold,
Further still from my dad? Is that where he
Really lived and the only place I might
Find him, since none of this can be made right?

The most important event in my life
Thus happened before I was born. You'll sense
This from many Holocaust children, rife
With too much meaning, straddling a fence
Of silence across a crater of strife.
It's the only way to maintain a defense.
Or else the parent talked too much — equally
Terrifying and difficult, really.

Why *do* the Jews stay Jews? "How odd of God
To choose the Jews." I never can recall
The comeback to that ditty.* Jews are mod-
Ern and ancient, open but with a wall
Round our way of life. Chosen for a job —
That's all. Don't Christians think Jesus was called?
Why is allowing for a pantheon
Threatening to those who allow just one?

Fending off the scary rest of the world
Plus my own muddy emotions, I am
A rock, I am an island, I am the world.
The Jews cause all tragedies: the Titan-
Ic, for one example. Not an iceberg?
Ginsberg, iceberg: same thing! It's too demand-
Ing to monitor everything. Let me
Stop here and allow you to go pee.

---

* But I *can* look it up. It's been attributed to Lord Alfred Douglas and Hillaire Belloc, although the actual author is one William Norman Ewer. One reply comes from Cecil Browne: "But not so odd/As those who choose/A Jewish God/But spurn the Jews." Leo Rosten added, "Not odd/Of God./ Goyim/Annoy 'im."

V. EZRA AND JOHNNY

1.

Having an utterly horny a.m.
How I love that word — horny — so teenage,
So uncomplicated by the mayhem
Of emotional petulance or rage,
The rage is to tear off clothes and lay 'em.
Like paranoia with pot, it puts a cage
Around other notions and single-minds
Me toward bed and men with luscious behinds.

Sexy stanzas are fun to write. But gosh,
It's no fun to do them for *no* reader.
Writers like to titillate. I can't quash
My desire to go public. The cedar
Of su penga plants itself in my posh
Loam. I think that you're cuter than Jeter.
Hope you don't mind him entering this verse.
You entering me makes all thoughts disperse.

Never has love been created better
Than under the tender touch of Johnny.
Where did he learn such angles, to get her
So enhanced, so expectant. My yoni
Opens, the sun embraces, the fetter
Falls, the stream plunges into the Swanee.
Even now, hours later, I throb, half-come,
Remembering his warm, insistent tongue.

And that is merely the beginning. Sex
Continues with his admirable penis
At play in the fields with the sword. O Rex
Pengum! Or Pengum Rex, if grammar is
Obeyed past rhyme. He tizzies me, inspects
His genius in the arts of Venus.
I'm in love with his dick, source of so much
Joy — but because joined to his brain and touch.

What a surge is sprung from good palaver!
To say a word I haven't heard in a bit
Or a usage that's fresh — ooh lah la, clever
Talk is like a tongue right on my clit.
Then the cream starts and talk becomes cadaver-
Like, no longer what I want: Talk to my tits!
Then your penga slides on in, and what I say
Is no longer smart (but that's OK!).

I put my fingers around my wrist,
Amazed that you're exactly as thick.
Gushing about your penga (biggest, finest)
Is true but is also (hard as a brick)
A metaphor for (longing to be kissed)
The unshed, unsaid personal (a lick!).
Complicated, ambivalent, puzzled,
Affectionate, warm, desirous, dazzled.

A line: "How a candle instructed me."
Perhaps I have never been quiet enough
To learn from a candle, although my knee
Swings wide when I think of Johnny. A rough
Shadow in the shape of your head shows me
A light, a flame of buoyant lust, a puff
Of smoke that spreads atom by molecule
Between us through all of air, desire's fuel.

Enough of arms and men! No, not of men!
Never, never, never, never, never.
Boy crazy am I. An ass like that of Ken,
Len, Pig Pen or Stanton, whenever
They flutter through my mind, tease me again
With longing and homage. They're forever
Mine, as all boyfriends and husbands should be
Mine. Don't they know they can never leave me?

I'm like the tiger, Byron said: If I miss
I disappear, but if I hit — crushing.
Is that a role model for politic-
Ians? Or would they be better like Russians,
Who smoke incessant cigarettes and hiss

At those who rule 'em, from czar to Prussian.
If politicians would just disappear
Perhaps the rest of us could think and hear.

Yes, those who run the country are corrupt,
A truism barely worth repeating; fair
To say you find that once you've drunk and supped
With them, your wallet comes out mostly bare
Of money and principle. Interrupt
Or quarrel, reader, to no end. Robespierre
Is one sample of a pol run amok
Causing many others to end up shucked.

Robespierre and *collaborateurs* — Marat,
And the lady who knit. Was she real or
Dickens' creation? A mystery that
I can't solve, at least not while Johnny snores.
There's history elsewhere than my husband but
Sloth is my middle name. Oh, it's a bore
For poets to get by on charm and wit —
D'you prefer the augenbite of inwit?

A.k.a., *The Prick of Conscience*, by Dan
Michel, who despite his jaunty name and book's
Suggestive title, did not bring a plan
Of fun to the fourteenth century. His prick looks
No more turned to joy and a gallop than
Those gloomy ghastly guys — Saints Stephen, Luke
And good ol' Augustine, who hated sex
As you'll know if you peruse his codex.

But back to Dan Michel and Robespierre too —
How easy to let rhyme swing you away
From the focus of your stanzas, "you"
Meaning me obviously, not to be fey,
Not a robust poet-girl like me — true,
One with stoppers I have to haul from the gra-
Vy, which sort of links to Michel's prick
Though getting my husband's *is* more Delphic.

Into philosophy's thorns do I go?
No! My beliefs are simple (and those guys
Inane): Be honest, past thirty forgo
Hating your parents, manage money wise-
Ly. And the thorns burn like bees. Let God fo-
Cus on the doubts. I can take care of mys-
Elf. Butting out of other's news the route
For rabbis, mad dogs, gen-X'ers and brutes,

Who give their thanks for absent Puritans,
The *Times* says. Did they report some were left
In New England still? Can they cure a ton
Of ills? The cussing that's spreading? The deft
Do better, the Wildes killing with the gun
Of pun and wit, while slower thinkers heft
Insults and sticks, but find it difficult
To dodge the rough shots of the catapult.

Just how well-read should a president be?
Asks the *Times*. Great leaders aren't always great
Intellectuals, says the op-ed piece.
Discernment and wheeler-dealer smarts rate
As more essential qualities (to me —
I read no more of that editorial prate)
As is having thought ahead to office
And so having been youthfully cautious.

Eat the rich, I often say (you know I do).
Not that they're so delicious but fat cats
Are force-fed, like veal calves, on costly dew
(No — that's models), roe and multihued plat-
Ters of delicacies, plus the sinews
And heartaches of the hapless. The self-sat-
Isfaction of the rich appalls. It follows:
We must indict those with a million dollars.

It's a lot of work to be poor, to scrounge
For money and be fed by rich people,
A certain kind of poor, that is, not loung-
Ing but unsung-artist poor, to be full
Of needs and fire, of brilliance and astound-

Ing ineptness and undesire to pull
A living as others do, with a job
You can go home from at day's end and fob

Off onto a heap, like a shirt you pull
Over your head — presto! your clothes are changed,
Maggie Dubris wrote, from cotton or wool
To laundry, thereby confirming that change
Is instantaneous. Distance/presence. Full/
Empty. Byron/other poets. Deranged/
Wage slave. Breathing/defunct. Being poor and
Being sans cash are likewise water/land.

Emerson said too much adversity
Is superior for the moral nature —
A true friend — to too much prosperity.
The problem is that the rich agree, sure
That *they're* uncorrupted, and poverty
Is elevating everyone else. Were
This true, how noble would be Africa
And Asia, how debased America....

Back to the guys ... in time ... next line ... maybe.
But let's talk more of Robespierre, last seen
Fucking Ms. Knitter, guiding the Navy
(Of whose Twelfth Fleet I often have been keen
To avail myself) and constructing avi-
Aries of messenger birds, France having been
Web-less. They didn't invent the Internet
So they refuse to say they'd prefer it.

Forget France! On to New York's East Village
Where Robespierre's a bistro in a basement
Frequented by children of privilege
Who're charmed by the Pepe LePew accent
Of over-well-bred waiters' sacrilege
Of school French wobbling in summers ill-spent
In Nice. They planned to be Rimbaud or Stein
But came back purveying meals with a whine.

"After great pain a formal feeling comes."
Is that what's sent me to ottava rima?
Beau so sick and suffering —his poor bum
Poked till that set in motion this scheme of
Dying. But not yet, doc says, so he'll come
Home, though he won't get well. His nurse Kareem, a
Kind Jamaican, pats his hand, gives morphine.
Get the patch not the shots, I hiss. The fiend,

Wanting drugs, or a furlough from my life.
When did I get too sedate to party?
When did the E.V. fill with nine-to-five-
Ers — in suits, no less! Why, my neighbor hardly
Is home, he has too much money, no knife-
Edge risks for him, he thinks we are tarty,
Sad old farts with little going for them
Like trollops glittering in cheap adornment.

Although you are distant by far from me
You are still so much closer to my bones
Than my own flesh. Your crumbling and crummy
Bones are locked away under a tombstone's
Hooligan embrace. My bones are dummy-
Silent. You — my love, my troubles, my moans —
You are not nearly far enough away.
You turn my flesh inside out for play.

"In the closet with the Fleece about his neck."
Everyone knows what that means for the land.
Here it's de rigeuer to make closet checks,
Maintain there's no point for gays to play hand
Close to chest since nobody gives a heck.
In fact, the more flashy the better, and
With the lamented death of Quentin Crisp,
The best banker add-on's not tie but lisp.

Quentin Crisp — the naked civil servant
Who I'm sure was quite as elegant nude
As a model as he was in turban —
No, more fedora, but always a dude
(Not cowboy but Edwardian). Observant

Thin English nose, bright ascot, cadging food
At Cooper Square diner, a free meal what
He seemed to care about most: the jackpot.

Bonnie and I saw him perform back when
I wrote about his show for her arts page
Of the school paper. He charmed the audience
With advice of the sort that appears sage
But works only for himself, a doyen
Of taste. I saw him on the street (his stage)
A week before he died. He swept past in
A proud trail of whispered recognition.

Enjoying your espresso at the bistro?
Let's go to my building, the Ezra Pound,
To meet characters out of the abyss, though
Who's there now is hardly the resound-
Ing cast of times past, when Phyllis so
Worked it — wait, no tales yet, a countdown
First, from One, where lived the Brazilian bombshell
Through Number Sixteen, where now lives Rachelle.

The Ezra Pound (not so much named for
The poet as cuz we like to say we live
"At the Pound") was "Lower East Side" before
The nabe got hip and fixed as "East Village,"
On Firsts Ave and Street and over Gringer's store.
Can you imagine a better site? Give
Me a million bucks, I'll stay where I am
In my tumbledown hovel, thank you ma'am.

It's by the subway, the versatile F train,
And the landlord, Michael, leaves us alone.
We haven't painted for twelve years, but the rain
Doesn't pour in at least. Room for our book jones —
Well, almost, since every spot, from windowpane
To toilet, is piled high. Even the phone
Rests on a stack of "someday we'll get to those."
Snug to be surrounded by the poets.

Our apartment's a classic tenement,
The size of an eggplant. The walls are thin.
When I moved in, I took off sediment
In many layers and languages — in
Polish, Spanish, Greek. One impediment
To repose is that our home is so min-
Iscule. Two people in one room so rustic,
It's a wonder we've not long since bust up.

Tub's in the kitchen, as the Pound was built
In 1910, before indoor plumbing.
Eventually, each floor got a toilet
But a serious legroom shortcoming
Meant no bathroom fit for a Vanderbilt,
Unless Vanderbilts like nude homecoming.
What price modesty? A private washstand
Would run up our rent each month by a grand.

Rather than renovate, we cover the tub
With a board, making it our countertop.
While, as I said, this place serves as the hub
For books galore, we have no room for mop,
Vacuum, table. There *is* a table — cov-
Ered with (hey, surprise!) books. Books and a crop
Of magazines, mail, more books and paper.
It's cozy and that makes me feel safer:

I like seeing all corners at all moments.
I like not having the option to shop
Or to replace my stuff with a pageant
Of possessions. It's wasteful to own a lot —
They're golden chains rather than a garment.
I even like that it's pointless to mop
As that's a giant waste of time. Squalor
Becomes me, except it prompts J's choler.

Oh dear — oh dear — how difficult it is
To tell the truth or even some small part —
Accuracy in a molecule's fizz
Would please me as much as to see the heart
Clearly and new. Any small expertise

Seems as arduous as bottling a fart
For uproar later. Here, let me begin
Describing my apartment once again:

Oh dear — oh dear — how difficult, my dear,
To progress from room to room, even though
There are only two. Curtains for the rear
Windows I got in Paris long ago,
Lace with pale flowers and a milkmaid who peers
Out at the photos and prints high and low
On all walls. A Ginsberg photo of Jack
Kerouac, three Schneeman-Berrigans, in black

And white, with Ted's great poem "10 Things I Do
Every Day." A rack of tapes, lots of shelves
(Mostly books), J's desk, my little desk too,
Boxes everywhere from a lack of elves
To complete renovations. We meant to
Put in a loft bed but inertia quells
Too many plans halfway, leaving a mess.
My responsibility, I confess.

When I went on a trip to Mexico
One year, I gave my friend John some paint chips.
I expected to come home to the glow
Of cool gray walls and dark gray trim. That pips-
Queak, eye inspired by my trip, let it go
Wild with yellow, pink, blue in random strips.
I was amused and rather than lambaste
Him, applauded his creative good taste.

2.
When you're a poet you tend to devour
Books. In my crowd, mysteries are in vogue
At random times, or folks are overpowered
By Arctic perils, English manners, rogues
Or biographies of Eisenhower
And the like. Chain readers, absorbing brogue
To burr, indiscriminately — what falls
In our field of vision keeps us in thrall.

Johnny's reading *A Deepness in the Sky,*
An eight hundred-page sci-fi novel. Best
Thing is the author's name: Vernor Vinge. Why
Do boys like sci-fi so much? Is it dest-
Iny or social expectation? I
Recall four guys I lived with who progressed
From gloomy *Dune* to Asimov's trilogy.
The girls skipped them. (Is it biology?)

Another gray day — what sort of summer
Is this?! And I have a mote in my eye.
Or a moat beneath, where tears flow. Bummer.
A word I can never use without my
Mind zagging to a Far Side cartoon (dumb
Maybe but fun): a deer with a bullseye
On his chest being solaced by a pal
Who's saying, Bummer of a birthmark, Hal.

Okay, six hours, get used to it, if that's
All I'm going to sleep of a night. Uncouth
As my days may be, it's these stupid vats
Of hours to fill. Hot kisses on the mouth
And elsewhere are what would work now, and pats
Up and down my torso, from north to south.
In spring, lovers linger in the soft air.
Pigeons scatter, squirrels skitter, horses stare.

My bed is piled with newspapers as well
As books — worse 'cause they're noisy in the night
When I move plus take up more room plus well
Able to stand their ground when kicked aside.
Towels too, that're piled there due to ceiling hell
(Will George ever return to plaster? Right
Now, doubtful.). I'd like to go back to sleep,
Wake up and write something that's much more deep.

Or I can try to write an even more
Inane stanza this morning — not to men-
Tion that I have but a few minutes for
It. Byron's *Don Juan* is quintessen-
Tially quick — yet vast. It's a gaping door

Into manners and women that he pen-
Etrated with his humor, ribald dic-
Tion and fast gallop along the Baltic.

Hey! Let's go be revolutionaries!
Right now! ASAP! What'm I wasting
My time with articles, functionaries,
Books?! My ideals are taking a pasting
While I watch baseball. (Distraction varies.)
But no more! No more cars! sex! or tasting
The delights of the world. Instead, improve
Things! Get some visionaries on the move!

But. There's a tower of at least a dozen
Books that I'm smack in the middle of read-
Ing, and more I hope to get to guzzling
If ever I have five minutes to feed
My head, extra minutes when I *am* in
A neat frame of mind — it's happened! — to weed
Trash out of the pile and my brain's engaged
Not in idle or mysteriously caged

Due to plowing through so many mysteries,
Which — have you noticed? — cheat by throwing in
New info halfway through a history
That leaves out crucial facts — "Oh, going in
Should I have mentioned that she's been mistrea-
Ted unto blindness?" the author says, again
Leaving out the scrap explaining the dick
Being a midget. It's all a bit thick.

Officially brain-dead, I've been too numb
To sit with much but crime stories of late
("Why" is another tedious tale.) Dumb
And tired, that's me. Ran out of 'em (hate
That) and started a book that's "real": *Death Comes
For the Archbishop*. "Easy" but it rates
As literature. I welcome vast stacks
Of similar books for further attacks

Of comatosity. Trollope and Twain
Would be there; Frank O'Hara and Whalen
I can pretty much always read in pain.
McMurtry saved my life once when failin'
To make up with Johnny, for three days main-
Ly read *Movin' On* till I saw hailin'
Distance of surcease. The book let me catch
My breath until I was able to hatch

A plan for us to get back disrobing,
Which we sure did. The ideal book to fetch
You out of grief needs to be absorbing,
Letting you off the hook for a short stretch,
But without being way too disturbing.
Kipling is perfect to capsize a kvetch;
Kim got me through a painful ear infec-
Tion. I'm always eager for FMF —

Ford Madox Ford, that is, of whom you will
Recall having heard as this poem moved along.
It's time now to climb over our hill
Of reading matter to see the Pound's throng.
We'll pop on up to the top floor where we'll
Stop first at Lucky's, who had lived here long-
Est when I first moved in. He was a gent,
A hardboiled cribbage player and a bit bent.

Lucky weighed eighty-four pounds, if that much.
We thought for years he'd been a Merchant Marine
Till we realized he could have been no such
Thing. Too small: He just liked sailors. Once Queen
Malu, a Spanish Jackie O retouched
By hormones and lighting, lurched past, not preen-
Ing for once but mad, threatening life and limb.
Nobody would open a door to him.

Lucky yelled repeatedly, "Hey, Malu!"
Until Malu paused at last and snapped "What?!"
Lucky sweetly asked, "Got a cigarette?" Who
Else had the chops to disrupt such a hot
Rampage? It worked too, stopped Malu in mid-spew.

Lucky! Hero of the building. He got
Our hearts forever: Until his decease
In '89, we called ourselves his nieces.

He lived on the top floor, next to Bobby,
Who often got drunk and couldn't make it
All the way up. He'd knock on my door, sobbing,
Maudlin. "You remind me," he'd cry and spit,
"Of the girl I once loved." As if in a lobby,
He'd pass out, come to. Next day in a fit
Of remorse, apologize, which (immense-
Ly true) was worse than the first offense.

I've lived at the Pound for thirty-plus years
Since '77, days of Dominick
The Rapist. You know, Maggie said, B— appears
Loose in defining consensual kicks
(It *was* the '70s), but she too fears
It was nought but rape. That thought makes me sick.
Drunks and rapists — you'll soon begin to think
We're not offbeat but a cesspoolescent sink.

The brightest lights are Rachelle and Maggie,
My best friends here. Rachelle plays accordion
And Mag guitar. A great poet, not hagi-
Ography but fact, vetted by adoring
Her work. R is brilliant too, not lagging
In talent. But success is a Gordian
Knot for one who's slashing into some part
Of fame. Untying takes time from one's art

While to snub it means no recognition,
Which brings with it wherewithal (financial,
Emotional) to stay the course. Volition
Plays a role in choosing circumstantial
Movement toward what begins with ambition,
Veers to comprehension of the substantial
Hitches in equalizing life and art
When dragged along in such competing parts.

Not getting it today. Must start my bath.
Johnny said, "Lie down here and you'll get laid."
I did but I didn't. A matter of wrath?
No — of food. We don't fight, we eat. He said
No time for both and the gym too. The path
To sex is not strewn with roses! I've made
A slip in leaving out sex for so long.
So! To it in a big way — Donkey Kong!

No, wait. It was Long Dong Silver — lame porn
That shocked because it came in the context
Of Supreme Court shenanigans. Shorn
Of milieu, I doubt it was highly sexed
Or would make anyone but a greenhorn
Blink, scold or look aghast. Was there some text
With the image? I refuse to look far
Into what Clinton did with his cigar.

Phyllis made her living mugging ladies.
She was over six feet tall, imposing
And mean: *old* ladies. She had a baby,
And a boyfriend she set on fire, supposing
Him beset by devils. Her maladies
Raged at Bill in Seven, composing
Tirades on his door: Bill, I'm GoinG to kill
You sOOn. Bill! I'm going to kill you soon. KiLL...

But she didn't butcher him, merely brained
Him with the pole from her door's police lock,
A metal rod that can cause immense pain!
He went after her with a pot and clocked
Her. She went to the ER, and we gained
Her baby for a few days. Then we knocked
On her door: "We've got your kid." "Oh," she said,
"I wondered where I left him." Now she's dead.

So many loved ones have died that I can
Barely stand to think about chopping things
Off prematurely (i.e. pre-death). Man
Alive is a potential friend. Love springs
Back from awful cuttings. I always ran

Away from farewells. I love you — these stings
Can be soothed, can't they? It's rather as though
The game goes into the twelfth — you can go

On but really only if the score's tied.
If something has changed between you, no use
In yelling that you're still playing. It's died.
It's over. The other team has cut loose,
Gone on to the next. It's over. So, sigh
And go find someone new. Does reducing
Parting to metaphor wipe out my moan?
I never thought I would be so alone.

People die, people die. I'm good at how
To deal — what to say, what to feel. This year
Has brought desertion as well. The bent bough.
The severed member. Are you buried near?
Prop up that staggeringly final "ciao"
With prosthetic passion. Didn't know I'd fear
Death less than a move to Denver. It's damn
Unsettling to be living on quicksand.

I'm trying to think of someone to talk
About who's not dead. Not Alison — she
Died of a brain tumor. Erik? I'm shocked —
Erik may be alive! In '83
He disappeared, leaving a dog unwalked,
A refrigerator with jars of pee
And tales spread by Ray-the-liar (now dead) (damn!)
That Erik was in the Witness Program

And everything we thought we knew a lie,
From true name to hometown (wasn't San Fran)
To owning a place in Chelsea. But why
Would Ray lie? Erik'd bustle over, stand
At my door, simper "Wanna make love?" eat pie
Still frozen. I'd say "sure." He'd choke. I'd hand
Him napkins. He'd scurry home. No one was
Let in there: piles of paper, loads of scuzz.

Erik cleaned houses. He one time survived
A sprained ankle by saying that he'd used
His key (having to pee). The owners arrived
Home and he got flustered and felt accused
By his presence. Out the window he dived
Rather than concoct some sort of excuse.
It's too outlandish to make up. Was pot
Involved here? I'll never know the truth, not

In this lifetime. Erik loved opera.
What's with gay men and opera? The falsity
And fuss of Carmen and Cleopatra?
Giovanni's drama, Siegfried's self-pity?
Bias, yes, but true too. An orchestra
Is great, though I like rock — my heredity.
If rock is my natural state of affairs,
Why can't the culture of opera be theirs?

Cousin Bip may well not be dead but he
Sure is crazy. He moved to the Virgin
Islands, never to be heard from, nutty
As the coconuts they grow, a burgeon-
Ing trade for a laidback place. Sipping Cutty
Sark whiskey, getting high, scarfing sturgeon,
Strumming guitars — none of that his well-bred
Life at the Pound, where he had cats instead.

One cat was Nikki. She was named Psycho
When she lived with me. She was scruffy —
She'd licked off all her fur. When that shadow
Became gorgeous, I was a bit huffy.
Bip combed her, brushed her and combed her, although
She wasn't renamed till she got fluffy.
I like cats and they like me, or I thought
So until living with one proved so fraught.

There lies the cat, the feline fluffs her tail.
There looms her dark broad back. Some residents,
Mice, that have scurried o'erwrought, caught in hell
That never with a frolic welcome bent
To thunder, showers or sunshine but hailed

110

Free hearts, free fur. The occupants resent
That much is taken, although much abides —
Crumbs, cats, rodents and cockroaches besides.

An accomplishment I thought I could strut
Was cookery, till I recall my mom
Also thinks she can whip up dishes but
She can't (and now she must never see this poem!).
My creations have come out gorgeous duds —
Spaghetti with blueberry sauce was lame
And baked watermelon turned into strings
Of pink plus vapor. A few other things

I've made were less ghastly but also less
Invigorating to prepare. Cooking's
More absorbing to talk about than mess
With — true of plenty, not overlooking
Most vacations, and excepting art, chess
And of course most obvious of all: fucking.
Talk is cheap and talk is dear and that's
The way to make my heart go pitapat.

I've never understood folks like Peggy
Who read cookbooks for sheer entertainment
And whose iceboxes are stuffed, not dreggy
Like mine (to me buying salt's an attainment).
Dining's best from delivery boys legging
Meals to the Pound. No more enlightenment
Is here on the theme of food preparing —
For me, disrepairing and despairing.

No, that's not 100 percent the case —
I did cook on one occasion a year,
When Maggie and I swallowed and threw taste
To the winds and invited friends and peers
To Thanksgiving feasts. Invitees were based
At the Pound — we started having them here
To include Lucky. (After Bobby died
He pretty much never ate, only cried.)

We wanted to feed Joe and Steve Carey,
Or more accurately, Marion, who slaved
On a feast not hers (she's a Brit), barely
Cared, yet was (and is) a trouper. Our fave:
The "margarita" stuffing she ferried
Over from Second Avenue. Steve gave
His loud, kind demeanor to every crowd.
A back- and front drop as luminous cloud.

Lucky always supplied his homemade borscht —
Or was it from a can? No, it began
With chicken broth. He added beets (of course),
Sour cream, vinegar, onion. You'd be a fan
Of his contribution if you were forced
To eat it, which you would as a gentleman.
Who else brought what? Once Tim cooked a capon,
But that is not something we should dwell on.

We used to have to eat these meals at noon
'Cause Mag worked at three. I'd get up at five
To shove the bird in. Back to bed. Too soon
Awake again. We weren't early-to-rise
In those days. A big meal at that hour ruined
Our appetites, and the food didn't thrive,
Such as my bro's chili with frozen chunks
Of beef, and biscuits that were knotty hunks.

Once we had thirty-four for a sit-down,
No paper plates or plastic cutlery!
An American Legion hall, the Pound.
Once you sat, you were stuck there. Butlery
Impossible — all food got passed. Don't lounge
Or lean. Latecomers set off a flurry
Like a wave hitting a wave, breaking,
Condensing, drawn in tight, overtaken.

Further cooking lessons with Elinor:
If you thought you could nuke carob to sof-
Ten it up, well, it chars. If you adore
Food, skip ahead — these tales may prove too awf-
Ul for your stomach. I can cook but abhor

Advice. I'd rather be inventive. Quaff
A strong drink and dinner will taste better!
It's adventure! Throw off your food fetter!

Shortbread! My sister Lindsay sent a box
To me as she does each year. Her shortbread
Pure butter, irresistible. She rocks!
She used to send loaves of banana bread
With nuts, chocolate chips and cherries. She squawked
When I handed it off to Eddie, said
No mas for you. This is better — except
I ate too much and to the gym I crept.

Coffee! Another topic we have not
Yet touched on. Why does my neighbor's Folger's
Taste better than my fresh-ground hazelnut
French-Colombian roast? The taste, it occurs
To me, is little like the smell, a net
That sweeps you in. But then the flavor stirs
You less, once you make coffee your groove,
Since habit adjusts illogical moves.

Is there a reason to eat liverwurst?
Wait — is *that* the philosophy I want
To get onto? I thought I was immersed
In the larger fundamentals — death, Dante,
Spinoza — yet here I display a Hearst-
Like sensationalist take that must taunt
Meat-eaters to defend their principles,
Vegetarians to dump their disciples.

Can I be grateful and also crabby?
Love humanity in toto, like Swift,
But curt with individuals. Abby —
My rabbi — is the person to ask. Miffed
Because my friend at the bakery, gabby
Jim, sold my *reserved* cherry pie. A rift
Of six months or twelve? I do permanent
Boycotts, but with friends, truce is imminent.

Why is Thanksgiving now so horrible?
A lovely holiday almost nonpo-
Litical, for feats and adorable
Friends/family. Nonetheless, the tableau
Is gloomy not sprightly, ignorable
Comments cause fights, people put on Don Ho
Records for fun and murder, people die
In November and December. I cry.

3.

How about a little weather break? My
"Guaranteed" two feet of snow is just cold
And a mere inch. That's like the old joke: Why
Are women so bad at math? They've been told
That "this" is eight inches. The sun is shi-
Ning somewhere else, and men are playing bold
Games with gullible women. I've fallen
And will again, no doubt, a million

More times. A blind spot stays blind. That's the breaks —
We get smart slower than what's invented
To lure us. We barricade off one fake-
Out only to splay our flanks so we're bent
Low with "kick me" loud and clear on naked
Need. Or we get smarter in ways that pent-
Up desire demands but doesn't, I guess,
Translate into much real-world usefulness.

How have giant pandas survived all these
Millennia? Their breeding and nurturing
Habits seem not calculated to please
A baby (cub? pup?). You see them perching
On a bamboo — cute — but mommas can eas-
Ily crush their tiny infants. Searching
For the jump, I get distracted by *Sci-
Ence Times* on coral. To pandas say 'bye.

What ends, ends at a definite moment.
But how often do we know at the time?
I knew it would be the last enjoyment

Of sleeping with X— (and it was sublime)
But nonetheless surprised that my potent
Guess came true. Boyfriends shouldn't be a prime
Example of predictions since little
In relationships is not a riddle.

When I was twenty I was terribly
In love with X— Y—, a recently divorced
Man of thirty-six. In the Arab League
Of boyfriends, I was disarmed. A tourist
In the country of heartache, Laramie
Became a chilly outpost of a forced
Education in exile and despair.
He detonated me into the air,

Where a lump or two recombined themselves
And in due time headed for Manhattan
Where they gathered with the rest (thank you, elves).
And then at last I met Johnny Stanton.
But some dirt on X— Y— might be delved
Into, before I sigh and abandon
Other men. Last night I couldn't recall
His dick, so I guess for X— Y— that's all.

There's Colin, who I call the Australian
'Cause he's rangy like all Aussies I've met,
Except for one, the *Post*'s bacchanalian
Dunleavy, who we interviewed for *KOFF,* (yet
Another rag you've heard about), his alien
Twang charming, his mates jealous that we beset
Him. Colin's a skater and lives in Four
With his girlfriend Kim. I can say no more

About Colin. In Eight is Ramona
(I bypass Five). "He-she-it" the landlord
Unkindly calls him, um, her. A bone of
Contention to neighbors, she has a horde
Of odd visitors, is known to phone a
Cop whenever displeased, she has ignored
All pleas and orders in regard to noise,
And brings home scary, malodorous boys.

4.

We're in Nine. Way back in '79,
There was a poets' theater festival held
At St. Clement's on the West Side. A sign
Of those times: actor-poets who could seld-
Om act. But we (me anyway) did find
It easy enough to disrobe. I yelled
And fainted and sang (in Ted Berrigan's
Clear the Range) — and there I was! Bare again!

Then in a sheer-ish slip, in Jim Brodey's
Play, don't remember the title, my sole
Line: "Calling Dr. Neemon!" I imploded,
Hand flung against brow, a strapping Tyrol
Nurse. Shelley Kraut ravished the roadies
Of the Siamese Banana Gang in old
Play *Chrononhotontologous*, tight teal
Gown, carried on Gang's shoulders, copping feels.

The point's that Johnny Stanton directed
Henry Carey's play and therefore we met.
I got to know him when I objected
To sitting in the back of his truck — wet —
When a bunch of us went to Connecticut
To clap for Dianne in a Bertolt Brecht
Play — *Arturo Ui*, I think. She was Bob's
Girlfriend at the time but acting jobs

Incite lust enough among the artistes
That when we arrived at the theater
Dianne (presently renamed Alex) had feast-
Ed her eyes on Julian, no amateur.
They soon married. And it seems that the yeast
Of love rose in Johnny. For idolater
He picked me. His love rose and he soon fell.
It took four years but now I'm in his spell.

Sweet and tough — the man sure knows how to ball.
I feel the muscles of your upper arm,
Devastating as emergencies. All
I know is your weight on mine, the karma

116

Of having met in the first place. I loll
With your astonishing weight in me, charmed
By admiration, desire plus of course vamp —
And (inevitable ending) me gone damp.

It's his twinkle (knowing he sure does know
How cute it is). It's the kiss, warm as fleece
And as soft. Soft, yes, but insistent, slow
But inevitable, so we don't cease
But go on, fascinated. It's the low
Jokes and high jinx; acknowledging the beast
Within; the riotous, well-described past;
It's even being amused when I'm sassed.

Scissors! Me too. Paper. Me too! Rock!
Me too. Johnny Stanton and I can't play,
It seems, cuz we only mange to block
Each other. Mr. Mystery. I can't say
What makes him tick. It's a bit of a shock
That I don't know how he operates day
To day. Love the guy, fascinated, so
I guess bewilderment's the way to go.

The clichés seem abruptly to apply:
I feel *incomplete when we're not meeting.*
'Most every *twitch,* 'most every *reply*
I not only prize but mine for meaning.
I *can't stand to be apart,* feel a sigh
Shiver me. *Why waste my breath in greeting
Anyone else?* I need to breathe your skin.
How silly and great. That's the shape I'm in.

> All in the early pearly
> When cloudy was the weather
> That misty-moisty morning
> I was your own true girlie.

> The smoky shifty shadows
> Of the early pearly
> When I was yours from dawn to dusk
> Your own true whirly girlie.

117

What I didn't know: Our life is a love
Poem. After we met, it took me four years
To fall for him, but it didn't take much of
Me to see he's moldy, i.e., it's clear
He grows on a person. With boxing gloves
We touched one another first, and have seared
And blistered ever since, verbal punches
That make us laugh and grimace. My hunch is

As long as we can laugh, we'll be o-
Kay. Boxing gloves in fact — he was my trainer
When I mud-boxed at Charas as a show.
Though I meant it, Rose the entertainer
Kept yelling, "Don't hit me in the face," so
It looked like the fix was in. Our stamina
(Or lack of) meant we fell at the same time.
How can one win if doing it as mime?

Sometimes when I fear we have grown apart,
I reflect on what could tear him away.
He could want to be boss, a Bonaparte
Of the household. He could take off one day
For a pack of cigarettes, loan a heart
To a novel stranger, forget to stay
With me in senility or despair.
I could drive him away with my short hair

Or should I say gray hair, against which he
Is unreasonably set. By me, bald
Is banned. It's easier to be bitchy
(Or blond again) than hirsute. Don't be appalled
At my shallowness. You're no doubt vigi-
Lant too about whatever you have hauled
Through your life. What is heavy to carry
You should fancy enough to (re)marry.

In fact, I know a couple who divorced
And then remarried. Kathy and Kevin
Year before last retied the knot. Of course
This seems glamorous to me, and heaven
To them, or perhaps practical, not forced

118

Into romantic mode. After seven
Years apart, they moved to KC to try
Again. Not try: This is it till they die.

You can be married and selfish, of course,
But it's harder. Perhaps people who live
Alone can't help but be self-centered. One source
Of thoughtfulness lies in having to give
In. Everyone deserves the chance to force
Their deepest needs to the front, elusive
As fulfillment often is. But the needy,
As one of Hendyng's proverbs says, are greedy.

I have sweet crushes on many right now:
S—, a cute kid, who adores me with an
Extravagant purity and a pow-
Er that men become unwilling to pan-
Der to until they get to be about
Ninety, and then are full-hearted again.
Do they feel they're giving up their freedom
If they give you a morsel of welcome?

Or is the trouble within us women,
In wanting what we should never expect?
"Prove to me, prove to me," a friend — him and
Others — used to snap at me. "You object
To less than fervor from all specimens
Of mankind." Well, yes. Yes, well, neglect-
Ed women over forty-five tend toward
Invisible. So as not to be bored,

We need better ways to shine in the world,
Quit wanting to be taken for twenty,
By which is meant attractive and furled.
Me, I'm not mute nor frail — I've got plenty
Of something. Do men want it? I think, curled
In their eyes, I see their discontent
At wasting a mouth they think should just smile.
When women smile for men, why are they hostile?

I love love and I don't mind romance.
I think the thing about Valentine's Day
Is the tiring, flowers-on-demand stance
So many people feel required to okay.
What good is love without ants-in-the-pants
Spontaneity? V-Day makes display
Required and thus insincere, even if
You *do* mean the hell out of your gift.

Johnny Stanton came through with a bouquet
And a note: Merry V-Day Ho Ho Ho.
It wasn't a card – just a note. You pay
When you skip, guys. Here's some free advice, no
Strings: Send the flowers to her at work — you may
As well know they're to impress friend and foe
On the job. C'mon, who really likes roses?
One year I got three bouquets — which poses

The question of. This year a fucky kiss
And a raincheck. Oh, a quickie too, that
Went by me so swiftly I almost missed
It. Ha ha. Marriage is like being at
A video arcade, part lucky guess,
Part skill, part hitting a new level that
You had no idea was even there,
Like walking outside into lamé air.

Johnny! Never have I met a man more
Super. He scrutinized me squarely
Then threw open every possible door
And welcomed me into his life fairly,
Not shoddily or in half-measures, nor
Too porously either, as though barely
Of the masculine persuasion. A man's man
'Nd a woman's dream. My Johnny, my Stan.

There's more to our marriage than sex, I reckon.
A system of fines/rewards enforces
Rules: five bucks to cry as a weapon.
Long-marrieds Bob and Shelley are the source
For a law to stop our being deafened

By screaming: "No Arguing Tone of Voice."
This makes us stick to the issue at hand.
Fights are short, fair and mercifully bland.

My father would be ninety-nine today.
He'd be dead by now anyway or so
Querulous and reduced it's hard to say
If my adoration would have held. Know-
Ing his time was limited made each day
Applauded. I feel that with Johnny, though
Simultaneously I plan centuries
Of memories, capers and adventuries.

I hear myself whimper. It is the thought
Of you coming toward me, gleaming, royal.
I wish to be naked before you, caught
In your acute light, transfixed in the coil
Of your boneless regard, the snake that fought
To crawl into a secret cave, loyal
To heat and a little more. Who would hun-
Ger for more when she has the rising son?

I'm feeling as goofy as a cartoon
To touch your skin rich as English trifle,
As warm and burgeoning as far-off June,
And too, I'm fired by your mighty rifle.
Though I half-wanted not to jolt the moon-
Glimmer of flirtation and to stifle
The down 'n' dirty... my hacienda
Is wide open to welcome your penga.

5.
Instead of sex, guess I'll do the dishes.
Couldn't get Johnny interested. Well, it
Is five a.m. It'd be delicious
But I also need to do a good bit
Of cleaning, take a bath, find a vicious
Killer in the pages of *The Pellet
Of Pearl.* Did someone say pallet? Divine
To go back to bed. Sleepy at strange times.

I once planned to write a work called *And So
To Bed,* full of literature, folklore,
The culture of sleep. I love to sleep, though
I'm not Olympic level anymore.
Why I don't sleep brilliantly, I don't know.
Madame Recamier, my grandmothers, who bore
Their babies at home in the family bed,
King Og in the Bible, Oblomov, what's said

On a deathbed. The book could be a comp-
Ilation — Thurber must have some witty
Insights. Mark Twain took along his bed, clomp,
On all trips. Did Tom Thumb have an itty-
Bitty bed? Ours is double, we like swamp-
Ing each other with heat and skin, giddy
With jokes and remarks so personal they're
Lying between us like a kiss's shared air.

Where does the day go? I have many tasks,
Like bundling the recyclable papers,
Finishing this mystery, dusting the masks
That were gifts from Congo, having vapors
About tidying our house — Johnny asks
That it be done. I'm thinking my capers
Might incorporate clearing the kitchen
Table, if that'll get him to stop bitchin'.

It's the three-three-three day of the year,
With thirty-three left to go. That's five 3s. So...
Methodical. Yes, dear, and do I hear
Meaning here? No, just that I'm pleased to no-
Tice this fact. If you lifted your eyes, dear,
Who knows what excitements you might see, fo-
Reign / domestic dooms / bliss: "He was smoking
A cigarette, and I was *smoking.*"

I believe in love at first sight, because
The first time I visited NYC
I knew in ten minutes it was the Oz
I was after in my many dicey
Moves around the country. I didn't pause —

Moved here straight off and knew the enticing
Would last. It has, it has. I feel the same
Today as I knew I would when I came.

Herewith some things you may or may not know
About the East Village: A man who wears
A cowboy hat is gay (he didn't show
Up from Texas). Two kids on my block bear
The first name Pinocchio (mean or mot?).
There are way more tattoos than anywhere
Else in the world, many piercings, but pink
Hair is out of favor these days (I think).

Shades are big in this part of Manhattan.
They are worn indoors and out, day and night.
Even my beloved Johnny Stanton
Wears 'em always. It's affected, and his sight
Must be affected — so dark he's sat on
Stuff he wished he hadn't. Hipsters (the white
Girls) choose black-framed glasses like Ralph Nader,
Clothes she wouldn't wear unless someone made her.

On Fourth Street east of B is a beauty
Salon called Don Juan. The name is painted
In flamboyant, graffiti-style "cutie"
Script with curlicues. I'm not acquainted
With the staff, but in the line of duty
To research have thought I'd step in. Tainted
With Byron as I am, I'm sure to be
Disappointed they don't dig his poetry.

Saturday night on a Seventh Street roof.
Perfect place to watch July Fourth fireworks,
Which I love because they're there and *poof* —
Gone, like clouds. The poor get their share; rich jerks
Can't enjoy them *more*. Extravagant frouf-
Rou and when they are finished, nothing lurks
But some haze. No do-overs, no reruns,
Merely an eyeball flash stunning suns.

On most Fourths of July Maggie and I
Discuss whether we can see the fireworks
From the Pound's roof. We argue and don't try
To hang with people whose apartment perks
Include a glimpse of the East River. By
The time we realize — once more — that we're jerks
Who never remember, it's too late to
Go elsewhere and we don't get *any* view.

One time, however, we rode our bikes down
To the Brooklyn Bridge; they held the display
Several days before the Fourth. The renowned
Gruccis ran it. No one there! A workday.
They cascaded brilliant waterfalls, crowns
And rippling skyfuls of color that may've
Been more striking than the Bicentennial
Blasts I saw hitching through Pennsylvania.

I have watched the tree in front of my build-
Ing grow to reach the third story. I've seen
Half the businesses on the block killed
By soaring rents, changed tastes, fire or venal
Officials. Goodbye to the Levee, filled
With poor hipsters not yuppies. Bye, machine
Shop and shoe repair and the workboot store.
Bye, Little Rickey's and waffle empor-

Ium. Edgar travel agency, if you
Need a good deal to the Dominican.
My landlord, Gringer's appliances, was new
In 1918. The roof's tin again
At the pet store, once a bodega. New
Deli's Abdul's (José and Finnegan
Went farther east, either to the lowest
East Side or the Island. Only the slowest

Stay or those too traumatized to explicate
Their requirements, or those unusual ones
Who like squalor or think it indicates
Moral superiority, who shun
Middle-class life, who authenticate

Only what they have to pay attention
To. Speedy Locksmith, funeral home (Ortiz)
The unnamed tattoo parlor (new), a cheese

Store (I wish). The Fourth Street guy shyly said
Of his new grocery, "This is my dream."
They come, they go — the Baltic is long dead,
Replaced by gourmet coffee. The ice cream
Shop has left. New Rage trinkets, the pothead
Candle store, the gastronome pet food scheme:
All gone in the steady substitution
That lies in our urban constitution.

I'm drinking the last teabag of green tea
From Chinatown. Is that nabe a ghetto?
Is the East Village? Did it used to be,
When artists self-selected themselves to go
Into poverty in tenements? Key
To seeing something freshly: Turn it o-
Ver, look upside down. Also a clue to
Empathy — do you know someone feels like you?

      (Everyone is a complete disappointment,
      John Giorno intoned. It seems that phrase
      Has become my own mantra. The ointment
      Of social intercourse: hypocrisy. Plays
      Well with others but with no anointment
      Of trustworthy consistency. It slays
      Me to stand tall, to have their backs and to
      Know I get little back, not a tattoo

      On their psyches, even their eyes are blind
      To the simplest effects, like a haircut.
      Hair as a window to the soul, a kind
      Of trivial self-mutilation but
      Socially acceptable. Don't I find
      Myself trying to "get out of a rut"
      With something new — a big night on the town,
      Chapeau, earrings — when people let me down?)

As long as there's hair on the human head
There's lack of hair too, as everyone must know.
My bald former darling — you *know* I said
Keep your hair if you want to keep me. Low
Foreheads I prefer to high, although dead
In the middle is perhaps best. That slow
Creep upwards, like the one-eyed cat peeping
In a seafood store, and I'll leave you weeping.

February again and this epic
Continues. Is there anything pertinent
About my daily life that I've neglec-
Ted to illustrate? There's the hurting and
Joy, the enigmas and changes. Deaths, sick-
Ness, quarrels, blizzards and uncertainent
Of every kind. When things get calm, I get
Antsy. A spanner in the works? Get set!

And the mournful sound of the barbarous horn
Wakes Johnny from his sleep with quite a shock.
It's his day off! From his dreams is he borne
Only to realize that he set the clock
When he could have stood in bed. Forlorn,
He quickly resolves it's me he should knock,
And we're off to the races, both amused
By our squabbles and eternally fused.

What's the difference between "brains" and "brain"?
Like to fuck your brains out, the saying goes,
But "the brain's a muscle," but "blow your brains
Out." If I had half a brain, I would know
When it's plural brains and when my brain,
"My poor, unhappy brains," can be solo.
No one is ever said to have plural
Hearts, though enough give two-faced tongues a whirl.

Slave of love, slave of freedom, stubborn thumb
Stuck in every argument. A zombie
In trouble. A tentful of lime and rum.
A tower on the moor. Sinister combi-
Nation of ignorance and facts at random.

126

Sherlock Holmes leads a bloodhound to Palm Bea-
Ch. Ford Madox Ford marries me in the night.
Byron drives me home in a bug-eyed Sprite.

Philip H—! I've lost touch — again! — with you.
Where are Cowboy, and Otto from Jersey
From the Air Force long ago? Bob D—? Bruce
The football player who didn't stir me?
Ted K— up in Maine, what happened to you
And your silences? Schoodic Sam — nursey
To a bunch of kiddies like you wanted?
Sherry? Sonnie? Sunny? Ollie? Haunted

Abruptly by a thousand names from the past.
Wouldn't I know if an old friend, loved one,
Were dead? My boyfriend of three years — a vast
Expanse of time in one's twenties — has gone
Missing too. After twenty years! I'm aghast
He's disappeared. Forrister, Max Preston,
Otto, Pam, Dale and Gus are some names that sped
Pictures, laughs and private jokes through my head.

6.
Because I can't be fired (I freelance),
There will never be a bombardment by
A disgruntled employee! Let's advance
To the work itself. As editor, my
Job's to make others look good. I fancy
Myself a behind-the-scenes writer's ally,
Or a beautician who fashions with words,
Sculpting beehives out of piles of absurds.

The article comes, wild as the Klondyke.
I try to tame it, plow and fence the range,
Reap its lines in cultivation, fond like
An aunt in seeing its best features, strange
Though they may be. A tidy blond dyke,
Elegant queen, come one come all. The dange-
R is confusing myself with author —
Thinking I know better in my hauteur.

All pursuits of my youth, it turned out,
I was lousy at. My roster of jobs
Is long — it took me ages to find out
I could like my work and also make gobs
Of money. Work I was bad at paid out
Less given my uselessness, and I prob-
Ably hated it to boot. I'm in luck
I've found work I like and pays decent bucks.

When I think of all the work that's in front
Of me this week, I blanch. Couldn't I hire
Some help? While I could pay someone to hunt
Down specific info, an entire choir
Can't think for me anymore than the punt-
Ed tune I've dropped like a crow. You can gyr-
Ate all you fancy but it doesn't make
You a dancer. Own a pen without fak-

Ing your editors into believing
You're a writer. Dear Hack. I use that term
Proudly. I'm a proficient hack, weaving
From one subject to another, perm-
Anently connected to none, teething
On one scheme, cutting into the next, merm-
Aid wriggling in one sea, then the greener
One across the bay. No one has seen her

Settle down. Journalists have A.D.D.,
Which is short for Attention Deficit
Disorder, except it's not as seedy
As you might think. Just because I don't sit
Still doesn't mean I can't deal with the tedi-
Ous as well as the new. My emphasis
Is on commotion not calm. Guess I am
Like a guy that way — wham bam thank you ma'am.

On December 23, Johnny Stanton
And I mark one more year of "wedded bliss" —
Term so unByronic it's in quotes, tanta-
Mount to breaking up with my mentor. "Is this
Poem the consummation," asked Anselm,

128

"Of your affair with Byron?" I'm shameless.
But how'd Byron sneak into this section,
One I began to praise the affection

Between J and me? He's tall, dark, handsome,
Irish, "a man's man and a woman's dream."
His brainpower is without question awesome.
His quips slip in and in, his eyes steam and gleam.
Johnny Stanton! I'd pay a king's ransom —
But don't let that spur anyone to scheme
A kidnapping, at least not till we've marked
The date with dinner and witty remarks.

His hardness and his softness, his smoothness,
The roughness of single-minded passion.
Lightning-fast reflex and lightning-sharp kiss.
Hearts that beat like thunder. Trembling, ashen
Before the gift. Riding the same wave. Bliss
And attentiveness. It's not in fashion
To speak of love like this, when twin tattoos
Display affection more than bills and coos.

When I think of Johnny, I get corny,
Rambling into thickets of silly grins
That steady as stares, while I get horny.
The hands start roaming, the lips part, the skin
Tingles, all that's on my mind is to forni-
Cate, which I do, we do, the sequence,
In retrospect, almost as alluring
As our attraction and love are enduring.

I'm making my marriage sound too rosy
To be believed. I admit: he's a jerk.
Obnoxious. Inconsiderate. Nosy.
I'm not perfect either. Some days I work
Too late. And. And. And. I dunno. Go see
Him about it. It's my poem and the perk
Is I'm its emblem. All kidding aside,
Each marriage has issues. Ours: Cyanide.

> The tyrant dies and his rule is over;
> the martyr dies and his rule begins.
> — Kierkegaard

How horrible when your husband won't speak
To you. It must be another woman,
Because nothing happened — he's not seek-
Ing respite after a fight. I summon
My sorrow and say, Why are things so bleak?
"I'm busy" is all he'll say, inhuman-
Ly cold. He came in reeking of raw fumes
At one a.m. Thank god, it wasn't perfume.

My husband adores so many things more
Than he does me. I'm sad. Why don't I clean
The house if that will win him back? That door
Is shut — in his house, it's not a pristine
Vision of a pure marriage. I'm sad. Poor
Me. The man I cherish prefers to lean
On me about dusting when everything
Could be bells that ring and birds that sing.

Our love is a rusted bottle, a line
I half-stole from Jim Carroll, the only
Line I liked in the *Poetry* magazine
Anthology. Most poems seemed phonily
"Poetic," with lame epiphanies that whine
Of ribbons. Jim's was both bold and homely.
Sincere and ironic. Our love has rusted
But is, I think, not entirely busted.

You could say he's a nap after dinner,
But right now that's oh-so-desirable
That you might gather that he's a winner,
Which he's not: no more than admirable,
If that. Or you could say he's got inner
Beauty but what good's an adorable
Isle of Langerhans? I'd sleep if I could,
Be good if I should, get laid if you would.

130

Right here in the city, much of the fight's
Gone out of me. Perhaps in the valley
Delphiniums flourish. Perhaps cool light
Flies around Maine. In some rusty alley
Topaz cracks open with the jagged bite
Of cornered cats. Blurred leaves count the tally:
One who lives on earth and remembers this,
And one who lives on a long-ago kiss.

Why would any self-respecting man want
His wife to give up her identity
When they marry? Why would a woman flaunt
Powerlessness by voiding the sanctity
Of her own name? A porous and daunted
Life as Mrs. Man — ancient fantasy
I am galled women fall for. Might as well
Bind the feet and lunge into Stepford hell.

Beautiful girls are generally more
Interesting than ugly girls because they
Know that they belong in the world; therefore,
They're allowed to take as much space as they
Want. And because people are prone to soar
Under the kindly attention of praise.
Oddly, the fatter one is, the less room
One is thought entitled to consume.

I don't feel like a stanza this morning
(Don't look like one either), plus short on time
As I woke up late, scribbled a warning
To my oaf of a husband. What's a rhyme
For "time," damnit? Can think about mourning,
Feel sorry for myself there too. No limes
Left, maybe no milk either. It's supposed
To rain. Will that douse the fire down below?

"The body carries on to its own / borders."
Oh yes, the body, it's high time I stuck
It in, right here. I'd say that the warders
Of limbs make a sharp line between my muck
And yours. I don't feel merged; even hoarders

Of deep feeling and deeper sex seem to duck
That final crossing. So perhaps the out-
Skirts are not vaguely drawn but are without

Clemency, without possibility.
I can never other than look through my
Eyes. You, cagey, and you, nobility
Snapped, and you, negligent even inside.
To speak in chorus shows agility
But not depth. I contemplate (with pride?)
My shallowness, so it's not any shock
To be as single-minded as a rock.

Johnny, Johnny Stanton, Johnny Stanton —
The man my sister Varda calls The Most
Handsome Stanton on the isle of Manhattan.
Right now he's being a bit of a roast
Pig. Odd how we still fight with abandon
After all these years — how little we coast —
How he's still Mr. Mysterioso.
I don't have him figured out — he's oh so

Curious to me and beyond my under-
Standing. While we're comfortable together,
I never know what he'll do. I wonder
If other couples work like us, whether
They are as flabbergasted when thunder
Follows lightning as I am when feathers
Fall from fowl. When I predict the denouement
To an issue I raise, I'm always wrong.

Thrones and even whole worlds have been upset
By a passing glance at a sheer leg,
Sheerly shorn of hair, morals and regret
For what's given up in order to beg
To follow that endless leg, both up it
And into whatever alleys and dregs
It may go. Women may want the same thing
But without thrones, can't give up everything.

When amatory poets sing their loves,
They often must jump back, out of the way
Of the havoc they cause. The cooing doves
Are loosed, and fly at each other like jays
Over baubles, ferocity that proves
The meek go un-mild when hormones sway
Their placidity. Are poets to blame
For the pimping that is done in their name?

Here's some more thoughts, works, poets and advice,
(If advice is what you want from confused
Me). I'd say that my guidelines for hitchhik-
Ing are generally sound, but to use
My counsel on poetry might be a vice.
Better to listen to Kenneth Koch, whose
"Art of Poetry" I take for my own text.
Better to read lots of poetry. Next,

Work out what the poets are getting at
(What you can lift from them, in other words).
Don't forget the young poets — read, cuz that
Is how to develop taste, without herds
Of antique notions stampeding you. Pat
Beliefs come when one knows before one learns.
Read a lot, write a lot, reject and embrace
In equal measure and in every case.

It's two decades by now since Jimmy Schuy-
Ler died (another on the long, long list
Of dead poets and friends — a fact that I
Hardly need announce at this point in this
Poem, eh?). His poems, even the long ones, vie
With Snoopy snaring soap bubbles in his
Teeth for transparency and lightness. How'd
He *do* that? Try it yourself and you're cowed.

It may seem easy at first — they're just lines,
You think, until you realize his tightrope's
Miles above the earth. His balance so fine
It's impossible to see that the soap-

Bubble is caught, let alone how he winds
It together. He said to me once, quote:
"I wake up, write a poem. That takes six minutes.
Then I've the rest of the day to myself." Wits,

Pay attention. "If the mind is shapely,
The poem is shapely," was Ginsberg's motto.
All your energy at all times must be
On poetry; *then*: "First thought, best thought." Oh,
I know that hint's engendered lots of ve-
Hement crap, but it's true you can't be blotto,
Ever. "Attention must be paid." And you'll
Be a poet then — trim and true, no fool.

It's been fun and useful to talk about
This poem. Helps me work through the technical
Problems, plus I bounce ideas and doubts
Off people. I feel solid as nickel,
Impervious to squelching from any lout
Who wants, say, obscurity; whose sickle
May be out to cut me down. But not Jack
Collom! who when I told him wrote me back:

       Dear Elinor, what *is* Ottava Rima?
       Famous Italian actress, screen and stage?
       Or drummerboy in '40s Louie Prima
       Bands? Perhaps a shape of parrot-cage!
       Or maybe it's a sort of crazy dream a-
       Bout a milkmaid in a total rage
       To gobble her peas and take her silver nose
       Discovering planets in their underclothes.

Driving rain, a violet thistlehead,
A red car, a woman in a red dress,
Both are red but different reds, one the red
Of Hawaiian sunset, one the heartless
Flattened color of berry jam on bread.
Rain flies horizontal, thistles confess
That Jack Collom's birds have always eaten
And Jack Collom's poems have never been beaten.

O King Harvest, with your face as grudging
As Stu Sutcliffe dumped from fame and fortune,
One-time Beatle, dead forty years, budging
For death but refusing to importune
Otherwise. King Biscuit and Queen Dudgeon
Rule in silly verse, headed for mortu-
Ary, sad and blue like a cat that fakes
Independence but wants the love that slakes.

Amazing how the days can be so full
And pass so quickly. My huge to-do list's
Never empty. It gets longer with bull
Crap and needments, magazines to read*, mist
To dispel, calls to make, solutions to pull
Out of half-baked ideas. Getting kissed
By Johnny is always and forever
At the top, Ay-oh-ay, ENJS ever!

I've decided to say that turning fif-
Ty is like getting an ugly, too-short
Haircut. A mortal fact you can but sniff
At and accede to. Can't fix or abort.
Just have to wait till it grows out and if
You can't stand it, you can't go to court
Over it. That leaves more time to anguish
Over other woes, or let them languish.

Friday I head off to Kalamazoo
To leap in with the medieval scholars.
This plan makes me face what I didn't do —
Finish college, in this case. Does knowledge
"Count" sans a degree? A gala haiku
Pretty much sums up my learnin'. Dollars
To donuts *you* don't care where or how long
I attended college, right? Am I wrong

---

* How come magazines invariably shoot
To the head of the queue, ahead of books
And work material and the gym? It's dut-
Y turned on its head, the short length that hooks,
Knowing you can read a piece in a toot
And a holler, lively account that crooks
Its human-enough finger. And swiftly it's
Time for bed. My cerebral life's the pits.

In thinking by now it doesn't mat-
Ter that I don't have a BA? I doubt my
Mother cares, if she even recalls that
I dropped out three or four times. I don't lie,
Just leave it off my résumé, my pat-
Ter does well in other directions, sleight
Of mouth that neatly cuts several years
So I'm younger too, which despite J's jeers

Is beginning to matter. Weird to let
An abstract (a zero, for heaven's sake)
Obscure my real and pleasant life. I bet
If I'd something to cry about, I'd take
Less time off to mope about this: If debt
Or death pressed on me, if a huge mistake
Oppressed me, I wouldn't have the attention
To watch the calendar with such tension.

"Petticoat influence" is a great reproach,
Quoth Byron, to whom I turn when I'm stuck.
I shall stop there, so as not to approach
Theft of his views (just his line). It's my luck
To be shaped by him, though whether it's poach-
Ing or homage is a topic we shan't tuck
Into. I'd love his speed, fluency, wit,
Lyricism — at least a bit of it.

I'm so heaped up with work that it's scaring
Me. How will I possibly get everything
Finished? I wake up at five raring
To go, or too edgy to sleep, zinging
Into Jack C's tape of yodeling — glaring,
Bizarre. A little goes a long way! Singing
Is only somewhat related — this sounds
Like munchkins on speed chased by smitten hounds.

Yes, this is life as we live it on First
Ave. I'm getting restless, ready to rock
Out. Although really, I Should Do Some Work.
A common remark, but I curse the docs
I edit. A man's trade brings out his worst

Qualities, Byron said. We'd rather knock
One back or light up or shoot up or
Take ecstasy, coke, heroin or uppers.

Each errand seems to take three days. It's sloth
But also busyness so extreme, pure
Torture to add to schedules with no slough-
Off time in them. Any plan for a cure,
Aside from quitting my jobs? No, I slosh
Around like washed-out galoshes, I'm sure
To keep on churning till the butter flows,
As an old Wynonie Harris song goes.

Right now this work's title still isn't set.
I tried *Don Juan A Poem* after John Clare,
Who, crazy, thought *he* was Byron and bet
He could continue that great work. His flare
Was for diatribe (and country life), his debt
To Byron was skimpy. Then I thought, Where
Better to get a title than from Byron
So I tried another form of *Don Juan:*

Don Johnny! (Greg Fuchs' phrase, I must admit.)
"Spare me," said Johnny Stanton. "Leave me out
Of it." Does *So Late into the Night* fit
With the comic element? It's no doubt
A lovely line from Byron's great, moonlit
"We'll go no more a-roving." Some sources shout
More secretively so I should shut up.
In fact, of this poem, this is quite enough!

Elinor Nauen has written or edited *Cars and Other Poems, American Guys, Diamonds Are a Girl's Best Friend: Women Writers on Baseball, Ladies, Start Your Engines: Women Writers on Cars and the Road,* and several chapbooks. *My Marriage A to Z: A big-city romance* will be out from Cinco Puntos Press in Spring 2012. She lives in New York City with her husband and cat. Visit www.ElinorNauen.com for more.